T0130220

SPEAKING UP FOR AMERICA

VAUGHN DAVIS BORNET, Ph.D.
Cdr. (USNR-Ret.)

Emeritus Professor of
History and Social Science
Southern Oregon University

IN COMMEMORATION OF THE OREGON
SESQUICENTENNIAL

SPEAKING UP FOR AMERICA

iUniverse books may be ordered through booksellers or by contacting:

iUniverse
1663 Liberty Drive
Bloomington, IN 47403
www.iuniverse.com
1-800-Authors (1-800-288-4677)

Because of the dynamic nature of the Internet, any web addresses or links contained in this book may have changed since publication and may no longer be valid.

Any people depicted in stock imagery provided by Thinkstock are models, and such images are being used for illustrative purposes only.

Certain stock imagery © Thinkstock.

ISBN: 978-1-4502-7796-9 (sc)
ISBN: 978-1-4502-7797-6 (e)

Library of Congress Control Number: 2010917672

Print information available on the last page.

iUniverse rev. date: 03/09/2017

Endorsed by the Jackson County (Oregon) Veteran's Advisory Committee on with this resolution:

"Recommended reading. This collection of speeches, now printed, reflects the signs of the times during and following the Vietnam Conflict and is worthy of serious thought even today."

DEDICATION

All but two of the fourteen patriotic speeches in this book were delivered before audiences in the Rogue River Valley of Southern Oregon beginning on Memorial Day, 1963, and continuing for some years on such occasions as Independence Day, Veterans Day, and Naturalization Day.

These orations *(for that old fashioned word describes what they really are) should refresh our memories on America's many wars for Causes. By standing up as patriots for freedom our countrymen hoped to improve the lot of humankind by triumphing over evil.*

This volume has been created primarily to memorialize America's growing array of veterans. It is especially dedicated to the service personnel who--willingly or unwillingly-- defended the cause of freedom in Southeast Asia during the painful Vietnam era. Especially remembered here are the dead, missing, and wounded from that sad war.

These pages display awareness that many during the Vietnam War used America's tradition of freedom of speech during those years to display their inner turmoil in public. They did this (while others mourned and wept in private) as the war dragged on interminably without declaration, satisfactory resolution, victory, or glorious consequences.

The thoughts expressed here were nearly all spoken in public between three and four decades ago; yet many of the ideas will be familiar. At the time, this speaker did the best he could to meet a need in a portion of Middle America. By offering them in this 21ˢᵗ Century I have an optimistic hope: I want my readers--those from the Vietnam era who are still living, those far younger, and observers in societies far from our shores--to be guided toward deeper appreciation of our United States of America.

V. D. B. Ashland, Oregon, USA

Contents

FOREWORD

This book contains speeches delivered by the author to a variety of audiences in the Rogue River Valley of Southern Oregon during most of the Vietnam War years. These words will be read in a new generation--this time following the year of an Oregon Sesquicentennial that remembered 150 years of statehood. Readers will often be reminded of our nation's long military history. Memories will return to the era of Vietnam—from the early 1960s to the mid-1970s. Great Causes will be remembered and gigantic wars recalled.

At this writing (2010-11) our nation lingers in Iraq and hopes to achieve goals and then avoid over commitment in Afghanistan. There we fight an enemy dedicated to tactics they call Terror. They do not discriminate between combatants and noncombatants, and they even rejoice at the prospect of death when attacking the United States and our friends. Verbal battles at home we thought to be long gone may arise again to arouse and divide us. We hope, perhaps in vain, that history does not repeat.

The words now printed in this book were sometimes prepared at the request of Veterans Organizations. Many were delivered (as I have said) on such patriotic holidays as

Memorial Day, Independence Day, and Veterans Day. Thus open patriotism is often visible in these pages. I am not in the least apologetic! It seems to me that Samuel Johnson was overly cynical when he proclaimed (maybe slyly?) that "Patriotism is the last refuge of a scoundrel." His remark is from an age when authoritarian rulers flourished, and there was little to be patriotic about. Since the old curmudgeon's edict does not intimidate me, readers will find on display here an unapologetic love of country.

The locale for these remarks was rural and small town Oregon--a pleasant place of mountains and valleys at the state's southern end: 290 miles from Portland to the north, nearly 400 miles from San Francisco to the south. Towns and places in what has long been called "the Rogue River Valley" are Ashland, Medford, Grants Pass, Central Point, Jacksonville, Ruch, Gold Hill, Shady Cove, Williams, Prospect, White City, Rogue River, Sam's Valley, Talent, and Phoenix. Substantial communities across mountain ranges are Klamath Falls to the east and Yreka to the south. This area is without doubt part of America's grassroots.... Yet withal, it is remote from America's population centers.

I certainly made the effort when speaking to include the Vietnam veterans with all the other veterans of our American military efforts. I believe that practice to have been uncommon. (There is no point in pretending that the Vietnam veterans were appreciated "quite enough" on Main Street when they came home. It didn't happen in cities or the academic world, but maybe it did in much of small town America.) As aging adults facing senior citizen status our veterans will always need comfort and appreciation from their fellow citizens, even when their major goal in battle—outright *victory*--was never realized.

As a professional historian I had some quiet misgivings at the time about aspects of the crusade America waged for years in Southeast Asia. I had no trouble, however, in recognizing the linkage between America's past and our announced purpose of waging a war to expand freedom overseas. When summing up a decade of national effort during a Veterans Day address in 1973 I was able to describe my audience as "relatives of those who died in our wars, surviving members of veteran's organizations, and citizens who simply want to preserve the memory of the soldiers, sailors, and airmen who served their country…." I then added, "There can be on such occasions a good deal of emotional strain…," meaning for audience and speaker alike.

Those assembling in Oregon's Rogue River Valley in that day varied from a few score of individuals to more than a thousand. The color guards were from home town units of the National Guard. They were our neighbors. Seated or standing before the speaker—who was occasionally in his Navy commander's uniform--were students, the very aged, the bereaved, the patriotic, and the young, a number of whom were in Scout uniforms. There were veterans and many who had read newspaper notices and just showed up.

At this writing, over eight thousand Oregon guardsmen have been serving in Iraq and Afghanistan. The happy return of hundreds of these in spring, 2010 was headlined news locally. Yet we are engaged in deadly serious warfare—as often before.

The ideas I offered beginning in 1963 were not normally targeted at furthering or hindering the military effort in Vietnam. American history was often my subject at a time when history was drifting out of fashion both in the school curriculum and in public discourse. I didn't debate how our Government chose to wage the War. My purpose was often to commemorate a patriotic holiday. It was to clarify American ideals and objectives. I hoped I was providing a counterweight to the sometimes ad hoc, even hysterical, sentiments being shouted then from various critics of our conduct. I felt that the increasingly strident anti-military outcry common to that decade was an unwarranted expansion of a dispute that ought to be strictly limited to the Vietnam effort itself. Fundamental attacks on the American system, I felt, warranted condemnation in public.

One extraordinary theme that permeates these speeches—but does not turn up in many public comments these days--is *apprehension over possible thermonuclear war.* That earlier generation remembered how the Pacific part of World War II came to an unimaginable climax. People were still in shock over the successful creation of a hydrogen bomb later by the Soviet Union—an authoritarian state that had come by 1960-70 to have hundreds of atomic weapons and the means to deliver them! Would we face total oblivion ere long from a nuclear attack? The matter was seldom far from my mind, for at The RAND Corporation for a half year in 1960 I had been the organizer and editor for six months on Herman Kahn's much anticipated book *On Thermonuclear War.* So it was that my speeches often concentrated on both the Southeast Asian war *and* the threat from a nuclear Soviet Union.

How did it happen that I gave all these speeches? *I was invited!* Before widespread color TV, community groups sought out speakers like me. Letters of invitation began, "Your name has been recommended to me.... We trust you can work it into your schedule." One just kept saying *yes,* ignoring absence of a stipend. These speeches came from a person with a scholarly and academic record and a military record as well. I had two decades of teaching and other responsibilities with the United States Naval Reserve in five widely separated communities. My job title had become Professor of History and Social Science, and Chairman of the Social Sciences Division, Southern Oregon College. My World War II duty spanned September, 1941 to January 1946 as yeoman rising to Lieutenant--in later years to Commander, USNR. My son, Stephen Folwell Bornet, also rose from sailor to Commander, USNR and served two years on the venerable *Yorktown* off the coast of Vietnam and beyond. (His father served a mere two weeks on CV-20, the carrier *Bennington,* adjacent to San Diego.)

*** *** ***

I wish to express my thanks to the surviving individuals who did the work of organizing the events at which these speeches were delivered so long ago. More recently, I appreciated advice on drafts of new prose in the book from Elisabeth Zinser, former president of Southern Oregon University, James Dean, former chairman of its English Department, legislator Jerry Barnes who is a dedicated friend of veterans, and several friends from the Ashland Rotary Club, Ron Bolstad and Don Stone. My son and daughter were helpful as the enterprise took shape and my wife Beth W. Bornet was, as ever, most essential.

Do permit me to recall my training at the hands of professors in three universities. Haywood J. Pearce, Jr. at Emory University taught me in cultured tones to love American History; he had a major impact on my mind and spirit. E. Merton Coulter, author of over thirty volumes on the South, chose to sponsor me at the University of Georgia, Athens the year before we entered World War II. Thomas A. Bailey, in his time a dean of diplomatic historians, was my teacher and mentor at Stanford University. His *A Diplomatic History of the American People* was long my bible, and I spent nearly two months helping edit his text *The American Pageant.* Bailey's teacher, Edgar Eugene Robinson, a major figure at that university for generations, was my major professor, and I worked with him on two books on the presidency.

*** *** ***

In earlier times speeches like mine were sometimes called *patriotics.* [Definition: *"Patriotic writings, speeches or activities; a display of patriotism." Webster's Third International Dictionary.]* On rereading these efforts in the perspective of years I am inclined to describe them as messages of affection, pride, respect, and memory. A focus throughout is our Southeast Asian effort's declared purpose, judgments often passed on it, and hopes vainly entertained by America's leaders. Earlier wars are often on my mind.

It should go almost without saying that with the exception of editorial corrections of the typo and clarity level these speeches are offered here as delivered. *Delivery back then was from clean manuscripts that had been carefully edited.* Even so, an island name has been corrected, several unclear references were clarified, a few tenses have been improved, an incomprehensible reference or a localism got modified here and there. Bracketed and italicized inserts clarify some things. My original manuscripts and an early booklet used in 1976 classes exist and are with the Bornet Papers at the Hoover Presidential Library. All in all the factual material of these speeches was not improved, augmented, or made clairvoyant in self-serving hindsight. One long academic speech was eliminated early on, and several speeches delivered from notes have been bypassed.

That some phrases and ideas in these *patriotics* will become part of familiar American patriotic expression is surely too much to expect, although I would like that. Realistically, I hope that reading these pages will evoke memories of idealistic struggles waged long ago by uniformed Americans on behalf of great national Causes— such as independence, thwarting an invasion, expansion to the Pacific, and accepting war to preserve the Union and free the slave. We would fight for defined freedoms and democracy in two world wars, and engage in half a century of Cold War. Next, we fought, by choice, various "limited wars" designed—it was hoped--to preserve and extend democratic government on our dangerous planet.

All in all, Americans have engaged in warfare time after time for purposes our citizens considered worthwhile. Personnel in uniform were drafted or volunteered to help the Nation achieve a variety of goals. All must know that *freedom* for ourselves and many others was not achieved without sacrifices and major costs. Somehow, we have managed during much of our national history to refer to ourselves as a "peace loving nation" even as we produced vast numbers of veterans from our many wars.

The author of this book has had from the very beginning the goal of bringing additional honor and remembrance to the American veteran, whose valor bought at great cost so many of the rights we have come to enjoy.

Vaughn Davis Bornet
Ashland, Oregon

MEMORIAL DAY IN ASHLAND, OREGON 1963

Delivered by invitation of the American Legion in the Downtown Cemetery, Ashland, May 30, 1963. A band played, and the speaker wore his Navy uniform as Commander, USNR. The text is the one delivered at the time.

Forty-two years ago another generation assembled together in this small cemetery to dedicate a Memorial Tablet of Oregon granite to the memory of those who had made the preservation of the United States their first concern.

On that occasion, there was agreement that such a monument should properly be "a permanent memorial, reminding those that come after us of the glory of the republic, the bravery of its defenders and the holiness of its ideals."

Those who then stood in this green and quiet spot seem to have found nothing incongruous in so forthright a proclamation, one that came from the lips of the local superintendent of schools, G. A. Briscoe. To them, it was entirely natural—and certainly accurate and proper—to state in public and before a gathering of adults and children the plain truth of the matter. And what was that? The United States is a glorious republic; its defenders had indeed been brave; its ideals were rooted deeply in Biblical wisdom and could be called "holy" on such an occasion without arousing undue surprise.

Looking back some forty years ago, on May 30, 1921, the War to Make the World Safe for Democracy was only 31 months gone. All knew that Armistice Day had marked the conclusion of a terrible war—a war of poison gas, trench warfare, machine guns, tanks, barbed wire, and unrestricted attack by submarines on ships carrying passengers, crews, and cargos on the high seas.

In Ashland, in the first two weeks after America's entry, 45 new recruits in "a wave of patriotism" joined the 1st Company, Coast Artillery, and in the third week 23 naval reservists left for Bremerton and active duty. An Ashland boy would soon write home from France:

"The part played by America in this war is one that makes a fellow proud of the old U.S.A. and thankful, indeed, that he was lucky enough to be born in such a great, wonderful country. And these sons of our country are doing themselves proud and fighting like demons. Many are the tales of bravery and devotion that one hears of them. The sad part of it is the many brave boys who are breathing their last in the fight against a cruel mighty nation."

The author of these moving words was a guard assigned to "strolling up and down a long dark post through the longer darker night." His personal assignment was small, but as he put it, "one must take that to which he is allotted and all these tiny efforts massed together make one mighty force that is relentlessly forcing the German military machine to its doom."

It was in 1898, a little more than two decades before, that an American president had taken the nation to war on behalf of the citizens of Cuba "in the cause of humanity and to put an end to the barbarities, bloodshed, starvation, and horrible miseries" existing in that troubled island. There is no reason why we should challenge the President's formal statement that we intervened in Cuba "in the name of humanity, in the name of civilization, [and] in behalf of endangered American interests which give us the right and the duty to speak and to act...." The local Jacksonville, Oregon *Democratic Times* wrote then of Spain, "A nation capable of gathering 600,000 old men, women, and children and herding them in towns and villages, surrounded by barbed wire fences and the most cruel and licentious soldiery on earth, where they can find nothing wherewith to earn a livelihood, and there let them starve to death, deserves no consideration whatever at the hands of any one." And the American Congress resolved "that the people of the Island of Cuba are, and of right ought to be, free and independent."

Memorial Day 1899, not surprisingly, was more generally observed than ever before in the town, with business houses generally closed, flags at half mast, and the national colors present (as the *Ashland Tidings* put it), "on every hand, in public and private places."

Buried in Southern Oregon are veterans of the Spanish-American War and of World War I; with them are often the loved ones who shared at the time their conviction that it was fitting that a great nation come to the aid of great Causes. Also to be seen in the cemeteries are the markers which tell us of the sacrifices of some who much earlier fought in the war to preserve the Union and which freed the slave. Eight miles to the north of Ashland are the graves of 17 who died in the local Indian wars of 1853 in the Rogue River Valley.

We do not now need to be reminded, for it is too soon, of the terrible cost in love and emotion, blood and sinew, of World War II. We remember Pearl Harbor, Guadalcanal, North Africa and Anzio; Normandy Beach and Iwo Jima; the fate of the Franklin and the Indianapolis. Later came a hundred thousand casualties suffered in the bitter cold of Korea. For some, the memories of all this are too close, too intimate, and too real to retell, even here, with emotional chapter and verse.

There were Ashland boys at Midway, at Wake, and at Pearl Harbor on December 7, 1941; the editor of the *Tidings* would write the next day that "America is… ready in spirit, in arms, in men, in fleet, in civilian aid, in production and in every other way required!" Here was surely overstatement.

Nearly four years later, Americans would be told that World War II had cost the lives of 260,000 men and perhaps $350,000,000,000. For every life lost by the nation in World War I, five had been lost in World War II. The 20,000 wounded of the earlier war had been joined by 650,000 in the next. "Yet I think," the Ashland boy had written from France in 1918, "that a man could never die for a greater country or a more noble cause."

With war's end emblazoned on page one on August 14, 1945, the *Tidings* editor spoke out for the home front: "Let's be thankful that we Americans were staunch and firm enough to face the hardships of war without any deep flinching—and to face any hardships that the early days of Peace bring without bickering and evasion of our duty."

From Washington, D. C. a few days later, General Charles DeGaulle gave a studied conclusion: "Without you, the American people, led by your great presidents, Roosevelt and Truman—there would have been no future for Europe or Asia, but intolerable servitude. Now we have to organize the world to confirm to the principles for which we all fought. In this immense task, the United States will have to play the leading part."

Gathered together in the Northwest as we are, we should still remember that if we were met near Lake Erie or New Orleans, near Trenton or Brandywine Creek, or in close proximity to Valley Forge or the Alamo, there would be a special duty to recall those who fell face down in the dirt while defending what to them seemed to be altogether "self evident."

It is in the American tradition, is it not, to display great courage when defending home and country? It has long been our practice to nail to the door our declarations of idealism, of conviction, and of hope for the future. We have fought repeatedly, as a great leader of our armed forces has so eloquently reminded us, for "duty, honor, Country."

Moreover, we have joined forces with, and welcomed to our side, nations and peoples with whom we have felt kinship--a community of purpose. On occasion, we have found ourselves on the same side with governments whose purposes in the world were (and often remain) seriously tainted. Some people were fooled then into seeing in the temporary wartime alliance with the Soviet Union a stamp of approval for Communism. But most Americans knew better then, and nearly all know better, now. (Détente can be a tactic but does not change fundamentals.) Will it not be our best course for the future to stand shoulder to shoulder with nations and peoples who appreciate and practice the healthy habit of democratic and representative self-government?

We face, now, life in a new world. We face also, inescapably, the need for a new brand of courage.

Earlier generations displayed the courage of action. Ours must show the courage of patience.

In addition, we live, and for decades perhaps, we are going to continue to live, in fear of a form of national disaster which may be all too possible.

If we are to survive such an awful ordeal of inaction, of patient waiting, of observing evil while unable to pull it out by the roots, we are going to have to live in the image and the shoes of our forefathers.

Our citizens are seldom going to be able to meet crises and solve problems as they once did: with daring action, heroic deed, gallant charge and direct sacrifice for a Cause.

The strain of the years that lie ahead may prove too much to bear. We may *act*—when action is unwise; we may show our courage in patterns which are technologically obsolete.

We may miss opportunities for great achievement in world affairs, because we fail to recognize the opportunity (or because we are unwilling to use methods little known to those who lived in a simpler day).

There are among us only a few whose knowledge of modern weapons, or whose awareness of changing patterns in political geography and international negotiations qualify them to lead our people into this new age. But there are still many among our people who stand ready to remind us that our history is something *special* in the world.

If we are to be true to our heritage; if we are to be in the future, as we have been in the past, a people idealistic in mood and aggressive against evil; offering protection to the weak and following our bent toward humanitarian aid for those in need; we must follow a hard and, indeed, a soul-rending course. On the one hand, Americans will have to pay tribute to a past in which large-scale military action could be considered an appropriate remedy for conduct which, on the world scene, clearly ran counter to the accumulated ideals of mankind.

At the same time, however, they will have to be able to adapt to—and to utilize—tools of negotiation, of conciliation, of persuasion, and certainly of reserved deterrent power which are not likely to bring the release and the outpouring of vital emotion that the declaration of war brought to earlier generations. On our entry into World War I, in 1917, Oregon's Governor James Withycombe could announce that "loyalty and patriotism are virtues which every true American is proud to possess and glad to express...." In his call for men to flock to the colors, he observed that "a spirit of patriotism not surpassed in fervor or intensity at any time in our national history lives in the hearts of the people of this great state of Oregon." Patriotism waited only "the call for expression."

It is a problem for the 1960s to find a way to channel the decent and praiseworthy emotion of patriotism into channels that will help—and not hurt—the United States as it lives on in a New World.

Unable to seek or achieve victory as on the battlefields of World Wars I and II; frustrated and angered as a result;

7

we may continue to turn toward invective, accusations, and too great a simplicity in analysis of problems and presentation of solutions. Unable, in a thermonuclear age, to destroy the enemy (with reasonable losses to ourselves) we may tear our society apart instead.

Those who once fought to preserve the Republic, to make the world safe for democracy, and to further the Four Freedoms, would not thank us for thoughtlessly tearing apart their nation and ours with violent invective, charges and countercharges, falsification of the record to serve immediate ends, and advocacy of *action* whose consequences lie largely beyond our control.

*** *** ***

Let us, instead, behave ourselves in a way which is truly in accordance with the words of the Ashland speaker of 1921, that is, "the glory of the Republic, the bravery of its defenders and the holiness of its ideals." Restraint in conduct, moderation in tone, and a decent respect for those opinions of mankind which are clearly rooted in respect for the individual—these are characteristics which will demand a form of courage worth having. We need and must have it.

Such undramatic and unexciting courage—the ability to give up one's prejudices and hatreds and fearful suspicions—will be vital in the awesome pushbutton and computerized days that lie ahead. It is never easy, moreover, to open one's mind to new knowledge and to new ways of achieving results in world affairs.

Courage less than indicated here will be a slur on the memory of those who showed raw physical courage in earlier years of wartime drama. Our motto might be, "They also serve who only stand and keep their heads." For it is a fact that time and technological change has destroyed all possibility of winning our way in the world with campaigns and battles to be fought in the manner of past wars. The possibility (and just maybe the reality) of limited engagements in remote jungles does not change the central picture except to throw it into clearer focus.

We cannot retreat from courage. We are the best hope, the only real hope the world has for reaching the distant goals of which man has dreamed through the centuries.

**** **** ****

OUR UNCERTAINTY IN HALF
CENTURY PERSPECTIVE

Delivered before an audience of elementary and secondary school teachers at Southern Oregon College during summer session, July, 1963. The speaker began his nearly half century life in Oregon the previous January. References to "the present" or the "present time" have been clarified with bracketed dates.

In 1928, I was a boy of eleven. Can it have been Only Yesterday? Actually, it is less than a half-century ago [from 1963]. It seems so far away: that world of Atwater Kent radios (no color television or multiplex FM, then); that time of the boxy Ford tri-motor airplane (not the 707, the DC10, or the helicopter); that era of the silk stocking (not nylon; rayon has come and gone in the technological centuries since the 1920s).

Also gone, but not forgotten, is the Dry Decade. Our government recognized neither the Soviet Union nor the propriety of "social drinking." The bootlegger was a big man, one with status in society. If some were even yet unsure about whether or not women should smoke, it was by no means because of any hazard to lungs or the cardiovascular system. (The Heart Association, Tuberculosis Society, and Cancer Society were tiny professional bodies; polio was a virtually unknown word among the public; the mental health movement was almost dormant.)

Any thought that tax returns would one day take so much effort to prepare would have been laughed at in 1928. The federal budget was balanced; the national debt was being paid off; and Congress saw no need to be in session during the terrible humidity of Washington summers. Half a decade ahead lay the alphabetical agencies of the New Deal: the TVA, the REA, the WPA, the NRA and the rest, with their expansion of power in Washington. The office of President was administrative rather than quasi-legislative; the Supreme Court had not yet been subject to 1937's intimidation from the Franklin D. Roosevelt administration; as it handed down its decisions it clung to tradition, that is, to law and judicial precedent as it performed its somewhat perfunctory duties.

The scientific progress of the 1920s was impressive to contemporaries, but to us it looks in retrospect a bit pedestrian. In mathematical computation it was by no means still the age of the abacus, of course, for the Dalton adding machine and the then amazing Comtometer were at hand; but the IBM Corporation, founded through multiple mergers in 1924, had not yet developed marketable punch-card equipment, and the 7090 computer (announced in 1958) lay far off with its storage capacity, calculating ability, and talent for offering results on paper. Maybe the questions being raised in 1928 were insufficient to warrant reliance on so sophisticated a mechanism! Thus: not in national defense (then immersed in trajectories of battleship guns);

not in retrieval of 70 million Social Security card records to help a system founded in 1935 that would not pay out a check until 1939. Higher mathematics resting on computers lay decades in the future.

The United States had only a tiny army in 1928. In the world of strategic thinking there had been only modest change since World War I. It is safe to say that most of the 651 pages of Herman Kahn's book analysis written in 1960, On *Thermonuclear War,* would have been incomprehensible and irrelevant to that earlier era. Words like deterrence, credible second-strike capability, and doomsday machines would have lacked meaning in the continuing age of the foot soldier, barbed wire, tanks, poison gas, and the concrete Maginot Line syndrome.

Our nation had abstained from joining the League of Nations, and there was little aggressive sentiment to become involved with that body. What would Calvin Coolidge or Secretary Kellogg think of our much later full support of and membership in the United Nations and its subordinate bodies; of the NATO alliance; of our commitments to succor Japan and West Germany if they should be attacked; or of the presence of hundreds of thousands of uniformed Americans stationed in such unlikely places as Korea and Okinawa?

Andrew Mellon, solidly Republican Secretary of the Treasury, was accustomed to a world in which Germany desperately owed reparations to France and Britain, while they in turn owed sizable war debts to America. Would he be at home in our post-Marshall Plan time of budgeting and finance—a world surely turned upside-down? In his day (1920s) there were few federal subventions to the states; no Alliance for Progress obligations; and no unimaginably costly planned race to the Moon and development of stations in space.

Back then, Japan was not yet able to take so huge a slice of the American motorbike market or flood us with TVs and radios. (We knew scornfully in those days what "Made in Japan" implied, and it certainly was not, then, precision cameras and sharp lenses!) Could Germany have scored so vast a success in remote American places with a tiny bug-shaped automobile? No, indeed; our Model A was innovative! German production was identified with Christmas tree ornaments and toy soldiers made of lead. Plastic lay far ahead.

Africa in the years after Versailles was a continent still dark, one filled with European colonies. Its political destiny seemed sealed for a hundred years to come. Who could have guessed that in the nearly twenty years after World War II alone there would be born no less than 49 new nations on this planet, with Africa getting its share?

As we continue contrasting 1928 with today [1963] we deplore the disappearance of independence in the Baltic area and the rise of new tyranny in Czechoslovakia, Poland, Hungary, Rumania, Bulgaria and others. An Iron Curtain has come, apparently to stay. Communism has triumphed in China. There are dictatorships in Libya, Uganda, and other "developing" states. Still, India, Pakistan, and Bangladesh have emerged. The British Empire, so major an entity in the century before 1914, is a shadow of its former self. The threat of both Central War and Limited War is taken seriously despite the United Nations, and "local" conflicts are being waged by armies or guerillas or madman leaders.

Much of the United States in 1928 showed that it distrusted "the Pope" and all his works, for Catholic Al

Smith faced a people far from convinced that full respect should be given to words from the Vatican. Protestant America had become content with versions of the Bible in use in the Anglo-Saxon world for over 300 years, especially the King James Version, with its combination of prose and poetry in melodious language. It had been memorized and memorialized by Cotton Mather, Abraham Lincoln, and millions in Sunday schools in village and city.

Surveying the world in 1928, experts in medicine and public health saw the basic problem of humanity to be in the need to eradicate diseases of old; the mere preservation of life seemed (in Asia at least) to be a basic need. John Earl Baker, a pioneer humanitarian from Wisconsin, expended American dollars and vast personal energy to feed starving Chinese in those years. Today, we point with quavering finger to the explosive effects of successes in medical research and of billions of dollars of expenditure in American foreign aid. The vast growth in populations long held in check by malaria, "the plague," high infant mortality, and famine has been both amazing and frightening. The "oil situation" and the "energy shortage" bring apprehension. Will they prove catastrophic?

Overall, one minutely examines the year 1928 and the 1920s in search of broad areas of contrast with our own day and finds more than enough to support the idea that *we live in a new age.* Oh, it may be true enough that man in the mass does not either sense or discern vast differences, but there is nothing new in this indifferent reaction to basic change.

Consideration of reality as it was then—and as it is now—brings reflections that disturb and even frighten. May it not be said that our Neo-Malthusian Age is one of fear that before the close of the century our planet cannot sustain us? Is there not latent but persisting fear that an exchange of modern weapons in our Thermonuclear Age will destroy all too many of us? Is there apprehension that our Democratic Ethic can neither subdue the Communist heresy nor even, perhaps, coexist with it?

In our own land is there not a sense that our basic morality is being pulled out by the very roots—perhaps, tragically, because of our permissiveness with youth, diminished ethical teaching in schools, and divided counsels? The rise of a women's liberation movement seems an amazing development—to men, at least! We sense that changes may be coming in race relations. Some who remember the conservation battles of Theodore Roosevelt's day have new fears, this time of those who may be on the road to destroying our planetary habitation with detergents, insecticides, weed-killers, and new products yet to appear. Yet "modern technology" might still save us, we hope. [Note: not a reference to planetary peril.]

There is entirely justifiable fear that the new processes, new automation, new wonder-gadgetry (like beams of light that can cut or plane or saw) may wipe out the lifetime employment capability of millions. At a time when some leaders decry the very existence of venerable public welfare programs, there is justification for the belief that programs to alleviate unemployment are bound to expand in the coming Age of the Displaced Worker.

The 1920s seem so long ago. How can we have developed so many, and such major, fears in so short a time as measured by the calendar? Was it really only 39 years ago that Robert M. LaFollette could get 5,000,000 votes as a native American radical progressive without being stereotyped as a "Communist"? What kind of an era was it that could have thought the minor economic recession of 1922 an important national disaster? Today, we face the implications of atomic energy converted to peacetime use; of food and fresh water from the vast oceans; of computers that can to a degree translate complex languages; of instantaneous world-wide television; of partial control of the weather----perhaps to our peril and not profit; and of a Space Age with all that such an age implies. We show concern over control of the oceans and their varied inhabitants.

It is too much for us to think on all this. Even though we have had a Depression, a gigantic War, and Korean War since 1928, it is actually only a little over three decades that have passed! We do have to call that earlier era of the Twenties an "*Age of Certainty.*"

By contrast, faced with all the changes we have noted, which came so fast and even accelerated in geometric progression, is it not legitimate to call recent years, our own Day, an "*Age of Fear*"?

All this, I regret to say, is my window on the world; it is the great contrast that over a half century has brought. And so we come back to my title today, which suggests (with merit, I think) that the year 1928 in the United States was really centuries ago. The time is now at hand when the historian may have to stop using the chronological units of old—the year, the decade, and even the word century— and must seek a new and more realistic measure, perhaps something like a "unit of *change*" in each of many areas of human activity.

If we were to apply such measurement to the time that has passed since 1928 we would find points of expansion and of compression. The unevenness would be disturbing in the extreme. At least we could not help but come closer to understanding the roots of our unease, our unrest, our disquietude, yes, and our *fear* as we contemplate where we have been, where we are now, and where we might be heading.

Where we have been calls for the services of the poet tuned to tragedy: from prosperity to long depression; from peace to world war; passage into the atomic era and the waging of Limited War without real victory (as in Korea and Vietnam). [sic] We are dedicated to "conquering" Space— not really a high priority when viewed in the perspective of mankind's history. Maybe it is now important to organize cooperative use of the planet's resources?

Where we are now calls for appraisal of so many factors as to defy hope of success through routine scholarship. We know that Americans have many material satisfactions to mitigate the cancer-like effects of so many fears.

Just where might we be heading? Who can say? In what condition--material, mental, and spiritual--will we be decades from now? Maybe it is just as well that we do not know.

Overall, the exercise of revisiting the year 1928 [from 1963] brings hope. Americans then lived on the brink of economic catastrophe but didn't know it. The event came; they survived. Then came World War II and new crises. Again: survival. Worse catastrophes may not come. If they do, we may survive anyway and be glad that we did— confident in ourselves and relying hopefully on our eventual destiny as a people.

**** **** ****

DETERRENCE, DÉTENTE, AND PEACE: MEANS AND ENDS IN AMERICAN FOREIGN POLICY

Delivered before the Ashland Rotary Club on January 2, 1964. My college president and dean of faculty were among those present. I had for over ten years been employed by famous non-profit research groups, including The RAND Corporation. It could be said I over prepared.... I made no effort to get this published, but I wish I had.

The United States in recent years has been in great danger. In some circles this bald statement has been accepted as true for even longer. Still, anyone who talked in the early 1960s with persons with standard educations making ordinary livelihoods can testify that the frightening danger to the nation was not routinely considered to be a credible fact.

There was abroad in the land some apprehension for "the future," perhaps; but it was typically a vague, distant future, a long way off. When, if ever, will the Soviets catch up? we asked. There is an unreality to such unrecognized danger. Few, even among leaders, were able to give a realistic description of the danger. There has been widespread disbelief accompanied by a sense of lethargy (even fatalism?) among our citizens.

I start from the premise that our danger may increase—despite declarations of détente, and in spite of our efforts to minimize it through seriousness of purpose, research and development, and comprehensive international diplomacy. That the danger will continue unabated seems inevitable.

If we are in danger as a nation, if our collective danger may be increasing and could continue to increase, the reasons are not far to seek. Our ability to guarantee our national survival and independence has been shrinking. Once, we measured national power in simple terms. How? We counted the number of men in uniform, the size of stockpiles of strategic materials, the quantity of machine tools available for quick production of a vast military capability, the extent of our natural resources, and the strength of our educational system.

There was more: Latent technology, the kind on which to rely in the later years of a war, was considered a national asset. Our manpower—firm in morale and familiar with the rifle; our historic spirit of nationalism and patriotism—such things continued to be measurable aspects of national power in the first half of the 20th century. Military reserve officers (including me!) studied such matters—or my case taught the course--under the book title, *Foundations of National Power*. Counting our assets in such conventional terms, Americans could say, in effect, "We *know* we are strong, and we know we have a vast potential for additional strength. If all else fails, we will win, even though it may take awhile." It was all very reassuring, was it not? Those were the good old days when we had self-congratulatory freedom from fear.

In earlier years, we now see, *time* was our friend. Ours was the Western Hemisphere, an area in which we were and would always be the one strong power. An enemy desiring to invade our heartland had either of two vast oceans to navigate. And that was the age in which the physical conquest of a nation by marching men was known to be the absolute prerequisite to victory in war. Two world wars were fought in that spirit.

An age of that type, so far as the atomic powers like the United States and the Soviet Union are concerned, is gone. Even so, it lingers on, unhappily, in the minds of senior citizens and far too many who aspire to leadership of their fellows. Why has it become obsolete?

In the total war of the future it may be that the winning power will not even feel the need to occupy the surviving territory of the loser! Violation of surrender terms will then be unthinkable.

It may develop that in the thermonuclear age the nature of war and the nature of time will become linked in a very real sense. The coming of intercontinental aircraft, first piston and then jet, was a warning blow to the time factor on which Americans had long relied.

The development of intercontinental ballistic missiles was the *coup de gras.* In some circles in the 1960s there was common discussion of a "one day war" in which victory or defeat would be definitely established. To what avail would be one's factories then?

It has become evident that in order to be reasonably safe in 1966, say, one had to take a number of complex R and D steps back in maybe 1956 or even earlier. There is a time gap, an all too real time lag between national strength, on the one hand, and the period of national preparation on the other. Lacking wise use of this time, as measured in years, one had little chance to be strong in any of the earlier senses in which national strength and national survival were measured.

In the 1960s, it was perfectly correct to say that America's enemies were in a position in which they could prepare for a new intercontinental war, but we would not know what they were up to until too late. We have had to presume the worst. Here was a staggering burden on those who plan and those charged with responsibilities. If the Soviets prepared properly in the mid-1950s, for example, they were likely to be in a more favorable technological and military position in the 1960s. If they did their homework in 1966, they were going to be strong in the 1970s. Thus it has become necessary to guess correctly about what the enemy is up to. Our planners cannot "go to the people" to ask what should *now* be done in Research and Development. The people do not know; the people cannot know.

Here in our own day, then, is a new international game. We might call it "Strength, strength, who's got the strength?" It involves who can prevail, given circumstances A, B, or C. Who has best minimized the risks? Our form of government in the United States, a democratic republic, is ill suited to this new way of doing things. We are used to having the people tell their representatives what to do to guarantee their best interests. But the people, literate by definition, are still unable to determine the true need (if any need) for a B-70 program, or development of a new type of radar screen, or new classes of ships equipped with Polaris. The experts have had to tell the people (actually their representatives) far in advance if the goal is *security*. Here was a strange way for a republican government to determine the destination of its basic budget, but it was what happened by mid-century.

Always, there have been highly placed citizens among us, ready and even anxious to cry out against even modest expenditures for the national defense. Educating these powerful and successful persons on reality has become difficult for those who have the inside track to unpleasant truths and unpalatable realities in technological development.

For Joe Citizen it has taken imagination to continue to support the Congress in its regular obligation to spend, spend, spend for the national safety. Many have just lacked such imagination. Others—well meaning, idealistic, friendly persons—have equated mere *possession of weapons* with the making of war and the advancement of evil. Few ideas are now more dated than this. The pacifist position has remained intact in morality and internal logic, but its applicability to a world complete with two major national powers like the USSR and Red China who are dedicated to total ideological conquest is hard to see.

The deterrence of nations of ill-will, and the very preservation of peace—even of the planet, perhaps—has come to rest on a new situation. It is not the *absence* of armaments in our hands, but their *presence*. Here is a harsh and very unpleasant truth.

Political figures have continued to pay lip service to arms control and disarmament, and there have been international conferences (SALT) *[Strategic Arms Limitation Talks]* to give headlined reality to the idea that with elimination of certain weapons (or proportionality) lies hope of final survival for mankind. All who know the history of international Communism's total dedication to world mastery find it impossible to believe that the Soviet Union and the Red Chinese will ever renounce force. Both believe in the use of modern weapons as legitimate means of attaining reiterated goals.

American expenditures for defense have had to compete in the open marketplace against champions of social welfare (aid, housing, medical care, scholarships), veterans' benefits, highway construction, farm subsidies, and internal improvements. Paradoxically, the higher the bill for weapons, the higher have climbed the costs in these other areas. For our citizens have reasoned that if the nation can afford such vast outlays for "unproductive" military items, then the more "worthy" causes certainly ought to get corresponding increases!

Some have said that if the nation can stretch to pay for expensive national defense, it ought to be able to spend in all other areas. This does not seem to be in the national interest, considering crises that may lie ahead. The leaders of the Soviet state have sensed that one cannot have unlimited quantities of both butter and guns; the American public has been slow to get the idea through their heads. Lenin, Trotsky, and Stalin said much about weaknesses they were sure were built into capitalist democracies. They would lack the will to survive, would they not? Americans at the grass roots may laugh at such a charge. When the time for courage comes, we would rise up like the Minute Men or the heroes of Iwo Jima!

The truth is that most of us lack the imagination to visualize or conceptualize—to bring into focus—the Great Problem of the Rocket Age: our own national survival.

Meanwhile, the leaders of the Soviet Union have continued to proclaim that their system will inevitably triumph, and they have continued to build a mighty war-making machine. Demobilization of some Soviet foot soldiers, when it came, was virtually an irrelevancy. The naïve overseas allow themselves to be encouraged by that self-serving reduction in Soviet foot soldiery. (It released rubles in mid-century for missiles, freed men for labor on bases, and showed Soviet reliance on the new weapons of destruction.)

Hopeful persons have also taken at face value Soviet assertions that their coming victory over the capitalist world would come through superiority in the economic area. The Communists said they would out-produce us and then out-trade us. Here was an assertion to be laughed at until a jarring wheat deal. Maybe the economic threat needed to be taken seriously! Perhaps a totalitarian socialist state indifferent to the welfare of its own citizens could indeed develop into a tough competitor. Whatever the prospect of any of this, there is awareness in high circles in America, and in both parties, that the military threat will still have to be treated seriously if the nation expects to live into the 1970s and beyond.

Why have most leaders in Washington continued to fear the Soviets? Why, despite the hope given détente, have they not been persuaded by the stream of olive-branch propaganda manufactured in Moscow for overseas consumption? Because *acts* belied *words*. There was the fact of the ever-growing military machine. There was the reality of Communist subversion and infiltration within most states—not excluding our own.

Americans have long carried the burden for the Free World. Because of geographical realities and the importance of truly modern weapons, the United States has become the only power in the world capable of thwarting Soviet ambitions. We take the Soviets seriously, because there is abundant evidence that the long oppressed and deprived Soviet citizenry stand four square behind their government's tough talk and tough actions in the modern world. There is little hope of hammering home new truths in the minds of the indoctrinated Soviet peasant and the misinformed factory worker. *[A pessimistic judgment of 1964.]*

We must accept the evidence that in the land of the Czars of yesteryear there has come to exist a dogma, a faith, a religion: the people and their leaders alike have said they believe in their system (but hope for improvements), and they act in accordance with their beliefs. There are few or no responsible American leaders, therefore, willing to count on internal upheaval in the USSR as a solution to our national safety. Hence we rely at this time on deterrence in fact and détente in vocabulary. We totally disregard unilateral disarmament.

Meanwhile, some who ponder world developments claim that belligerent states have mellowed with success. They say that producing shoes, TVs, cars, and telephones, etcetera might make Soviet leadership less ready to take risks pointing in the direction of new conquests. Surely, it is said, aspirations for more democracy and recognition of individual worth cannot be kept dormant forever in Communist places! Won't *time* solve this problem? Possibly, but will there be enough time?

The Communist ideology, Marxism-Leninism, is a tough bird. Over six decades since the Czars have not brought mellowing of a kind that is related to the problem of world peace of mind. Can we let down our guard on the thin theory that the bear has chosen this decade, this year, this month, to dull his claws? Upheaval can come from the inmates of conquered states in Europe and elsewhere. The Red Chinese have problems with domestic tranquility, and governmental problems exist from Indonesia to Thailand.

Thus I would argue that unilateral disarmament is a dangerous futility, especially lacking ironclad and enforceable conditions to guarantee the nature of the final outcome. There must be significant Soviet roll-back, getting rid of weapons of first importance.

When we talk or think of "disarmament" we must consider all of the kinds of threats we have to take seriously. The kind of disarmament that can bring relief to the frightened people of the globe will take a lot of serious study and lengthy negotiations. The same is true of arms control. We must not be rushed into agreements on the production and placement of offensive and defensive weapons, for we need mature reflection. The mere presence of arms in our modern world is not in itself a harbinger of war. Where one's opponent is filled with ill-will, the mere absence of weapons in a ready status brings war closer. Much depends on what is controlled, when it is controlled, and why it is controlled.

We are not ready for foolproof enforcement of arms limitation agreements. Here is an area for work, and insiders recognize this. Enforcement is an extremely important matter. It requires many skills, and these are found among specialists. We lacked such personnel in the 1950s, and they are still in short supply. We are short on persons prepared in technological knowledge and linguistic skills, who are ready to live for months and years in an environment filled with antagonism from those being inspected.

Nothing is to be gained, however, by pulling away from arms control. *We need full and continuing discussion with the Soviets—and with the Red Chinese.* With such discussion we may come closer to being able to bring the day when some arms control, with enforcement, will be possible. Limitations on testing in the atmosphere and below ground were useful early steps, but they were simple compared with what lies ahead. There remain missile sites, radar nets, hardened emplacements, secret weapons, materials for chemical warfare, and the rest. Still, an agreement on bacteriological war was a start, and agreement on hostile weather modification should be possible.

The very word "disarmament" is used here as roll-back; the words "arms control" as cut-off or plateau. The term "arms limitation" means agreement to stop building at agreed points. As we discuss what to negotiate with the Soviets, it would be helpful if we distinguished in words and meaning between rollback, plateau, and building up to firmly set terminal points.

Much has been said and written about peace strategy. *Peace* has even become an academic field here and there with a full bibliography and vocabulary. Let us make a few points on this. First, deterrence clearly cannot rest on either future or long past research and production. Today's deterrence will not be resting on weapons not yet in existence. We hope for future experiment, technological progress, and clever invention, but will all that prove too late? Nevertheless, we will be anticipating those things if we expect tomorrow's deterrence to be realistic. As we dedicate ourselves to cutting the national budget as time passes, we hope that *research* will not be the first to go.

As war was waged in the past, it was common for new weapons to be conceived of, developed, and built during the years of actual war. Now we are deeply into a period when technological change is such that a major war may have to be fought to its conclusion with the weapons and the defenses in being at the very outset of hostilities. True deterrence must be relying on what one has, and with what one can research and develop in the time available before tomorrow's finale turns up.

Building and keeping an effective deterrence force in the last quarter of the 20th century will undoubtedly consist of building and rebuilding, researching and developing, then going through it all again. Some among us claim we are safe because we possess mighty weapons in stockpiles. It takes more than that. Talking of "overkill" as we budget can kill us, however. Where now are the B-36, the Regulus, the Thor, the confidence we showed in air raid wardens and Nike sites? Repeatedly, we will be abandoning expensive hardware that seems perfectly good. Those bombers lined up near Kingman, Arizona and the ships floating at Philadelphia Navy Yard and Mare Island, California—after old victories—may be as nothing as compared with what may have to be scrapped. Waste such as Dyna-Soar may make our hearts bleed.

Make no mistake: today's Minuteman will join early models of Polaris in the junk heap. Wonder weapons do become obsolete, unable to do assigned jobs. The public will have no choice but to stand for this. Weapons must deter credibly—or not at all. They have to impress the Communist leaders, not the American voters.

Extreme lovers of peace and anti-militarists who say weapons and war are one and the same to them are going to have to join in *[taxpayer]* suffering during the long pull, unless they want American independence to disappear in the coming era. After all, the absence of central war during the past decade [spoken in 1964] has surely been more attributable to our possession of well engineered weapons than any other single factor. If we are lucky this peace with our major adversary may continue. We don't really know whether a disarmed world, so to speak, would stay at peace or go to war if armed only with World War II's weapons. Contrasting with this, a world armed for modern war seems likely to stay at peace or risk major disaster on both sides.

Do we really have a choice? We have no voice in the Presidum. We don't have a pathway to Soviet classrooms, where falsehoods about us are routinely taught and lifelong hatred for America may be engrained. Vast numbers of Soviet citizens may like us anyway, but what of their leaders? Do we really have any way of changing this?

It is my contention, therefore, that we will all have to look on expenditures of multiple billions of dollars for defense in the same light as other expenditures that make life endurable: spending for highway construction, improvement of education, subsidies to farmers, and aid to the aged. Defense, including the ability to strike second if we have to, has become a permanent part of our national posture. Survival is now part of our social security. The money we spend for weapons has become a routine part of the cost of living in a world that others, and we ourselves, helped to make during a quarter century of war and peace.

Above everything, *we must control our fears and subdue our passions*. We must work constantly to make sure that our nation, while it may be armed to the teeth, clings anyway to its basic heritage of decency and humanity. We must not fail in this. If we do, we will also fail to retain on our side the nations and peoples who share our belief in the perfectibility of mankind and in the possibility of guaranteeing perpetual peace.

**** **** ****

AREAS OF AGREEMENT IN AMERICAN FOREIGN POLICY

Delivered before the Retired Teachers Association of Jackson County, Oregon at the Girls Community Club Building, Medford, on Sept. 24, 1964. The version offered here is the one slightly edited for a second presentation before the Retired Telephone Workers of Jackson County several weeks later. (Oct. 12, 1964)

The American people have long been divided over the nature, purposes, and methods used to implement our foreign policy. Ask any man in the street. He will tell you— with vehemence. Yet despite this there remain some areas of basic unity in our foreign policies.

Thus, we refer at times to a bi-partisan foreign policy. What we are saying, in effect, is that on some goals and on some means there has been and may still be fundamental agreement—at least among people of good will and those who know the world as it is (and of course those who know their history).

I think at the outset that most Americans now agree that our national security rests and needs to rest on the possession (but not necessarily the use) of military strength. We believe that we ought to be able to deter aggression and if need be defeat it at any level of intensity. We want to be able to prevent attacks, whether they are nuclear, with conventional weapons or guerrilla warfare. Some among us do not agree with what has just been said, because they are pacifists who do not believe that countering violent aggression with weapons is moral.

Among those who reject pacifism there are disagreements over how far we should arm our allies, with what kind of weapons, and over how much freedom they should have in their use. Nor is it generally agreed that our armaments industry should sell to such an array of eager customers. Most seem to concede, however, that our collective security should rest on collective strength in NATO and elsewhere. There is, of course, sharp disagreement over the proper size of the defense budget.

Americans appear to believe in a considerable degree of economic partnership among the nations of the West. In Europe, Asia, and North America, there has been much cooperation, and many wish for more. Ever since the inauguration of the Marshall Plan in 1948, we have hoped to see a healthy economy in Europe; we were distressed when things deteriorated. Americans have wanted the Western economy to stand four-square against the Communist bloc. Most of us want an Atlantic Community with flesh and bones, not just a community of ideas. Since the Germany and Japan of World War II are gone, it is essentially new nations using the old titles that exist. We want, and we know we must have, their friendship. Economic partnership is our policy. We differ in how much and in what manner—not on whether to seek it.

We want, in the next place, to further our version of "revolution" in the World: *a revolution of freedom.* We want change in even the most backward nations. We would like the developing nations to achieve self-respect and self-government. We want them to be prosperous and happy, possessed of at least some self-sufficiency. We differ on how far we can go in trying to help the economies of others without hurting our own economy in the short run. In any case, we appropriate dollars to the Agency for International Development and put effort into the Peace Corps and help United Nations agencies and projects--all with the idea that we are aiding humankind while thwarting Communism. We do not agree in borderline instances. Among those would be Tito, perhaps post-war Vietnam, Angola, Spain, and Warsaw Pact countries. Please note: those wholly out of sympathy with our policy of extending foreign aid to many emerging nations have not been able to hold a permanent majority in the Congress.

The rational citizen cannot calmly contemplate the consequences of abandoning our aid policy at this point in our history. Aid is rooted in the self-determination doctrines of Democrat Woodrow Wilson; in the humanitarianism of Republican Herbert Hoover; in the good neighbor concepts and Four Freedoms concepts that emerged in Democrat Franklin D. Roosevelt's time; and in the post-World War II foreign policies of Harry Truman. The Marshall Plan was a creation of Truman's day. The two administrations of Republican Dwight Eisenhower pursued aid formulas in seeking a better world. The policy of friendship to yesterday's colonialized areas of the globe seems likely to withstand even the most heavily financed attacks of those who feel overtaxed, the isolationists, the nationalists, and the heartless among us.

We see, in the words of the Department of State some years ago (during the Kennedy Administration) the gradual emergence of a genuine world community. This is by no means the same as saying that we want an end to our American sovereignty. It is merely to say that we have sought the strengthening of international law and of world order, and an end to chaos in the relations among nations. We seek the creation of a world in which the whims of rulers or the aggressive designs of misled peoples will not prevail.

Look at the record: we helped to establish and we worked to develop such bodies as the World Court, the World Bank and Monetary Fund, and other international institutions (while not always leading). The Alliance for Progress and the Organization of American States were our doing. The Colombo Plan, the U. N. Economic Commission for the far East; SEATO (Southeast Asia Treaty Organization); ANZUS (treaty between the U. S., Australia, and New Zealand); CENTO (Central Treaty Organization of the Middle East); plus bilateral defense commitments—all are evidence of willingness to look outward (sometimes with caution). There is a General Agreement on Tariffs and Trade (GATT). And some agreements have been negotiated with the Soviets (atmospheric and underground test bans, cultural exchanges, ACBM, SALT) even if arms control negotiations have seemed endless.

We have seen mutual advantage in a world with some aspects of organization. Leaders of both parties have felt this to be the case. Jefferson once urged the practice of "peace, commerce, and honest friendship among nations," and all believe in this principle. But we have certainly come to reject in our shrinking world the rest of his phrase, that is, "entangling alliances with none."

Some speak of a future "community under law." Immediately, there arises the question, "But what of today's United Nations?" An official State Department document admits that the U. N. is an "imperfect instrument" as it stands; the Charter needs amending. Among problem areas are the voting procedures in the General Assembly; the composition of the Security Council; the overall problem of financing activities; the powers of the Secretary-General; the composition and functions of the U. N. peace-keeping forces; the philosophy and activities of UNESCO; and the controverted practical question of to what extent our aid dollars and goods should funnel through the U. N. instead of being given by us directly as foreign aid.

On such matters we cannot but disagree. Some want a strong international organization that matches the expression "world government." Such a government would destroy national sovereignties and bring "world peace through world law." Others have urged that the international body of the future should consist only of the nations of the free world. Still others cling to the status quo, defending today's United Nations. They defend its form and its every move. With the zeal of converts or parents, they are certain that it cannot survive change or modification. They do not explain, I think, how our own Constitution (the best the Founding Fathers could agree on when framing) has been amended over two dozen times to remedy defects and to bring change. But most Americans, I surmise, seem to want an organized international community of some sort.

One more idea on which our people still agree, perhaps, is the determination to persevere in the *quest for peace.* This means that our American people, says the State Department, will "strive tirelessly to end the arms race and reduce the risk of war, to narrow the areas of conflict with the Communist bloc, and to continue to spin the infinity of threads that bind peace together."

All Americans stand for the simple and Franklinesque idea of "try, try, try again." All except a lunatic fringe want *peace.* We all want to decrease the danger of war. Together, we fear modern armaments. We wish that our safety did not depend on the catastrophically frightening weapons of possible attack and defense. There is agreement here, is there not? But when such attitudes are translated into disarmament and arms control negotiations, when they lead to argument over proper action in a Hungarian or Cuban crisis, an apparent harmony of viewpoint may break down utterly.

Still, we nearly all recognize that we are faced by an alien system, by an alien way of life, by a philosophy (even a "religion") that is hostile to all that we are or hope to be. [*A reference to international Communism.*] While we do not all agree that rollback of the Communist world is a viable policy, almost no Americans suggest that eliminating the power of Communism would be a mistake. We do want to eliminate Communism! To that extent, at least, we do not really favor coexistence with that System, except as a very last resort. We all rejoice that détente has at least decreased invective in high places and facilitated the movement of individuals.

There are new organizations and leaders among us who say, in effect, that if we in the democratic world are to survive, we cannot and we must not, countenance coexistence in either the short or the long run. Some want permanent brinksmanship. These persons hope that the Soviets, the Red Chinese, and their fellows will inevitably retreat when they see our military handwriting on the wall. If they guess wrong, well, there will be an exchange of atomic weapons!

Our policy in recent years, on the contrary, has been to narrow the areas of conflict. We try to avoid conflicts that might inevitably escalate, and to reach agreements whenever possible that will *decrease* the possibility of atomic catastrophe. In spite of this official point of view, we waged "Limited" war in Korea and now in Vietnam, whatever the risks. And illustrative of the fact that ours is not a policy of abject weakness, Polaris submarines patrol the North Atlantic; our fleets are poised in the Mediterranean and the Far East; our Strategic Air Force remains alert. We have not shirked our duties in Berlin; we confronted the Soviets in Cuba; weapons development continues; and in Lebanon and Taiwan we have thus far saved our friends from attack or total convulsion.

We stand, in our American bi-partisan foreign policy, for the development of a world in which aggression will be obsolete; for a world in which all peoples will experience orderly progress toward the traditional goals of mankind; and for a planet on which war is ever more improbable. We will do what we can to make all peoples self-governing and happy as they freely live out the appointed span of their personal lives. Here is where we take our stand.

As we face forward in our formulation of foreign policy, we must be aware of fundamental changes in the international environment in which we think and plan. Let me mention a few areas in which failure to grow in our understanding can bring setbacks.

We have long lived with the presumption that there are going to be both Communist nations and free nations—and that our task is chiefly to confront "the enemy" and work to convert the uncommitted to our way of thinking. We have come to realize that the Communist world is far from monolithic except in its detestation of the capitalist world. Now we see that the uncommitted nations may well go their own ideological ways, avoiding the injunction we once posed that they choose *freedom* or *slavery.* Barbara Ward long ago envisioned a world in which the lineup would be between the rich nations and the poor ones. In her view, the economically and militarily evolving Soviet Union seems to have emerged as a rich nation like ourselves. In world standards it approaches "affluent." It is possible that the poor nations will come in time not to embrace either the Communist world or ours, but decide to shun or scorn— even hate—both the USA and the USSR, even both of their ideologies. Currently, the Red Chinese pose as a leader of a "Third World," although the similarity between their situation and that of, say, Botswana, is nonexistent.

The future is bewildering. Is a gigantic federated state ahead in Africa? Can we assume a permanent NATO alliance? Would life in a non-nuclear world really be safer? Will the development of an ultimate weapon (a Doomsday Machine) come into the picture someday to confound our policy makers and render obsolete overnight a United Nations of severely limited powers? Can we agree on territorial boundaries in the oceans, limit the dumping of pollutants, and further birth restraints? *[To help with overpopulation.]*

What I am saying is that in the world of the coming Seventies we cannot mouth the slogans of the past. We cannot postulate that change will be *gradual*. We cannot define for all time who will be our "friends" or our "enemies." We live in a new world to be sure, but before long that new world will become an old one. The facts on which we have long relied may in some instances cease to be *facts*. (The myth of unlimited resources in the world is already dead.) And the heritage of the past on which we would like to draw, the guidance of great men on which we would like to lean, may prove either inadequate or unreliable.

We cannot take our American foreign policy out of the realm of party politics, for in a democratic state there must be room for disagreement at the polls. We cannot silence those who criticize existing policy in its details or its major aspects. We do all need to sense, I think, how far we have come: the vast areas of agreement on objectives and the consensus on methods, which now characterizes the basic foreign policy of the United States.

We must keep ourselves well-informed. We must be attentive to our needs and opportunities. If we keep our heads, we will somehow manage to coexist with the apparently permanent fear of sudden catastrophe that is to be our companion through the years to come. The realization that while much divides us, much also holds us together, should help our morale as a nation as the years unfold.

**** **** ****

OUR CAUSES AND OUR FEARS

Delivered on Memorial Day, 1965, before an outdoor audience of veterans and their friends and relatives at the U. S. Veterans Administration Cemetery, White City (near the Veterans Domiciliary). Vietnam was on the speaker's mind. It was in that year that College historians Doug Legg, Betty Harbert, and Bornet formally briefed Governor Mark Hatfield on Southeast Asia and limited war at a three hour breakfast at the Bornet home.

Memorial Day, 1965 finds the veterans who live at Camp White thinking in terms of John Howard Payne's lines (now set to music). "Be it ever so humble, there's no place like home." You remember the first stanza:

"'Mid pleasures and palaces though we may roam, be it ever so humble, there's no place like home.
A charm from the sky seems to hallow us there, which, seek through the world, is ne'er met with elsewhere.
Home, home, sweet, sweet home! There's no place like home! There's no place like home."

We thought for a time that we might have to say, with the poet William Cullen Bryant, "The melancholy days are come, the saddest of the year...." Instead, as we look toward the future, we may rejoice with James Russell Lowell, as he wrote:

"And what is so rare as a day in June? Then, if ever, come
perfect days...;
Every clod feels a stir of might, an instinct within it that
reaches and towers....
And the eyes forget the tears they have shed; the heart
forgets its sorrow and ache;
The soul partakes the season's youth."

We owe a full debt to the soldiers, sailors, airmen, marines, and other fighting men we honor today. Our American ancestors who wore the Nation's uniform, and the close relatives and friends who wear it today, all have a claim on us.

What we owe, and what they are entitled to claim, is our continued loyalty to the great Causes for which they died and are dying. What are those Causes?

In Korea, where we had 157,000 casualties, the cause was the freedom and independence of small nations; that is, their right to exist free of aggressive conquest from their neighbors. But this was not all. Because Korea was at the time in the care of a United Nations Commission, so that our forces fought side by side with men from other free nations under the United Nations flag, the war involved the very principle of international organization for peace.

In World War II, that vast global conflict, we stood across the expansionist path of a Japan determined to control all of

China and Southeast Asia. We also sided with the democracies against the dictators—Hitler and Mussolini. Most Americans recognized full well in those years that we had nothing in common with Dictator Stalin of the Soviet Union except that we fought a common enemy. The cause of the West was by no means the cause of Red Russia. We were to discover in the post-war world how much this was so.

We fought, then, to destroy the concentration camp ovens of Hitler (though few knew it), and the "water cure" government of Mussolini; we did not fight to give a victorious Stalin a blank check to power in Europe. The Soviet armies, it turned out, did not at the end leave the countries of Central Europe, but this was neither our plan nor intent.

We fought for and talked about the Four Freedoms, and we dreamed of a community of nations. We hoped for permanent peace. These were our Causes. They are still our Causes. The evil of fascism has given way to the evil of Communism. Each evil has been backed by mighty nations armed with mighty weapons. The tools of war and the force of twisted ideas have stood behind their past successes. Treason among Americans was not responsible for the successes of Hitler--nor of Stalin.

We must not waste our energies and divide our people with fruitless accusations and a useless quest for traitors or scapegoats, armed only with the uneasy feeling that all has not gone well in the postwar world.

The democratic governments we were promised—in Poland, in Czechoslovakia, and elsewhere—have not been created. But this is not *our* doing.

Were we unwise in our statecraft? Were we unrealistic in our use of land armies in Europe? Did we trust in conferences

45

leaders who had amply demonstrated that they were not to be trusted? Perhaps the answer is "yes" in each case. But this was human failure—not "treason." It is dastardly in the extreme to charge our commander-in-chief of those years, the head of our chiefs of staff, and the commander in our armies in Europe—with dereliction of duty—totally without proof. Some pamphleteers have done this, writing sleazy tracts for free distribution. Throwaways pretending to be newspapers, both despicable and disruptable, have been spread around, even here in our very midst.

If we are to honor our dead, we must not dishonor their memories by throwing mud and garbage on their leaders and their causes.

Consider World War I. Looking back nearly fifty years into the past, we recall the belief of Woodrow Wilson that we could have a war "to make the world safe for democracy." We were sure that German militarism could be crushed for all time. We were wrong. We believed that small nations might come to enjoy the luxury of self-determination. The vast oceans, we thought, might be free. Diplomacy might be conducted through open covenants openly arrived at—as Wilson said. A League of Nations, some agreed with him, might enforce peace.

America entered World War I, not just for economic reasons (the debts, the munitions sales, the linkage with the solvency of the Allies); not just for reasons of race solidarity (the kinship of language and of literature, of religion and of common history with the Anglo-Saxon world). Nor was it from a sense of gratitude (the distant memory of Lafayette and the French treaty of 1778). Certainly it was not from a desire for aggrandizement: to build a colonial empire or to dictate the terms of the peace. No.

We went to war in 1917 because of the German submarine, because of the sinking of ships on the high seas and the wave of emotional response which the American people felt at the Kaiser's violation of what we considered human rights. We believed Germany to be the aggressor in the European war, and we deplored what had happened in Belgium. We did not enter war only in a spirit of vengeance. Rather, we followed the idealism in words and ideas of the one of a kind orator in the White House.

President Woodrow Wilson's words when he faced the Congress on April 2, 1917 rang clear then; they have pertinence now. Let me read a few sentences:

> "...It is a fearful thing to lead this great peaceful people into war, into the most terrible and disastrous of all wars, civilization itself seeming to be in the balance. But the right is more precious than peace, and we shall fight for the things which we have carried nearest our hearts—for democracy, for the right of those who submit to authority to have a voice in their own governments, for the rights and liberties of small nations, for a universal domination of right by such a concert of free peoples as shall bring peace and safety to all nations and make the world itself at last free.

> "To such a task we can dedicate our lives and our fortunes, everything that we are and everything that we have, with the pride of those who know that the day has come when America is privileged to spend her blood and her might for the principles that gave her birth and happiness and the peace which she has

treasured. God helping her, she can do no other."

We fought for our principles and our dreams. Alas, our dreams were shattered, and the causes for which some gave so much did not prevail. But the great vision of Wilson in those years made a permanent impression on leaders at home and abroad. The principles did not die with the Armistice, and we must not kill them at this hour in our history.

Going back: in 1898, we fought for "*Cuba Libre.*" The war is little understood today. Tyranny, in the person of the Spanish general "Butcher" Weyler, could not be allowed to endure only a few miles from our shores (it was said). We did win Cuba's freedom from foreign domination, and we rejoiced. But a half century of Cuban history has shown that freedom can only be permanent where a people hold it higher than all other things. The nation that gave Cuba its freedom longs for the day when the Cuban people will again be free.

Thirty years earlier, the War Between the States, that great civil conflict, saw the soldiers of the Confederacy fighting for independence and the soldiers of the North and West fighting for the Federal Union—against "Rebellion." There are few in this nation who regret that the slave was freed and the Union preserved, but we still know the cost.

Our magnificent nation, stretching from the Gulf to the Canadian border and "Maine to California" sometimes seems to have been preserved to act in this century as the savior of a democratic Europe—but it was a long time in the coming.

Maybe it can be said, in addition, that our Union—strong, and rich, and humanitarian—was preserved to cure the sick and feed the hungry and drain the swamps and serve the cause of democracy in the second century since the end of our Civil War?

Many soldiers who fought under the Union flag at Vicksburg and Missionary Ridge and Gettysburg saw their cause as freedom for the Negro slave. For others it was the Union. We still fight for freedom for all Americans. The struggle for a more democratic America is a Cause we should remember on Memorial Day, for many who died fighting for the stars and stripes saw clearly that the Negro could not forever be a slave in a land dedicated to freedom.

Our first war, the struggle for American independence, was fought under a proclamation that all men are created equal and that government should derive its powers from consent of the governed.

As we contemplate what course we should follow in Vietnam, we need to reexamine our history. *We need to recall why Americans have given "the last full measure of devotion."* We need to consider the risks we have taken in the past. And we need to weigh most seriously the effect on the national moral consciousness if we now abandon what we have been. Can we betray what has made us what we are?

We cannot, of course, reform the world. We cannot change age-old ways in a single generation. There seems little prospect that we can do anything very effective or dramatic about that part of the world which rests behind the Iron Curtain and the Bamboo Curtain. But in the rest of the world our physical power and our moral leadership can still be exerted. And they can be effective.

Contemplate our past. Consider the Causes for which we have struggled. Especially, consider the record of recent decades. Since 1945 we have risked the consequences of the Truman Doctrine in Turkey and Greece; conducted the Berlin Airlift; and fought the Korean War. Other risks we have taken include the landings in Lebanon, and the building and alerting of SAC [Strategic Air Command] and Polaris and Minuteman. We constructed NATO in spite of Soviet threats, and we have a global network of alliances. We have shown our willingness to take acceptable risks to defend the heritage in which we believe.

As we ponder our present and future course in Vietnam, we should certainly reflect upon the risks already taken. Our future course will not be straight as an arrow nor clear as crystal even if we do this. But we will have the confidence that we have not carelessly, casually, or thoughtlessly betrayed what we have been and what we have long believed.

Always, we must work for peace. We must believe that peace is infinitely better than war. This means that we must be convinced that our weapons were designed and produced and deployed for deterrence—not for use. We are armed to keep the peace, not to bring wars. But if, through self-deception and misjudgment of our ideological enemies, we somehow come to lack the courage to defend ourselves with modern weapons, we may in some crisis perish as a people and a state.

We must hold peace high. But for the present we must not fear the worst—or we may bring adversity on ourselves. The present and the future are frightening in the extreme. Yet we must not lack courage. We must not forget the Causes for which we have long struggled. If we know our

Past and keep it green, we will be keeping faith with those who wore our uniforms in the Past. Our American fighting men, living and dead, are entitled to no less than this.

**** **** ****

SOME FUNDAMENTALS OF
THE AMERICAN SYSTEM

This short speech was delivered in Circuit Court Number 2 in Medford, Oregon on November 16, 1965 before an audience of perhaps a hundred. It consisted of several score of individuals being naturalized from many countries, their friends and relatives, and representatives of community service organizations. So it was a Naturalization Day. A copy of my address was given to each new citizen to read and keep.

Nothing should please a citizen more than the opportunity to discuss and to praise some of the fundamentals of the governmental system of the United States of America. Just what is it that can be said, in a very few words, to a few of the thousands who, like the handful of Vietnam refugees, continue to seek out this country as a place of permanent residence?

This is a nation of, by, and for the people. One of the great books about this country is *Democracy in America*, written in the 1830's by a Frenchman, Alexis de Tocqueville.

This is a work to be recommended to one and all, a classic on its subject. In chapter nine the author remarks that he has now examined the institutions of the United States. He writes of laws and the nature of "political society." It became his opinion that "a sovereign power exists above these institutions and beyond these characteristic features which may destroy or modify them at its pleasure—I mean that of *the people.*"

In America, he continues, the people appoint the legislature and the executive power, and they furnish the jurors who punish all offenses against the laws. I will quote him:

> "The American institutions are democratic, not only in their principle but in all their consequences; and the people elects its representatives directly, and for the most part annually, in order to endure their dependence. The people is [sic] therefore the real directing power; and although the form of government is representative, it is evident that the opinions, the prejudices, the interests, and even the passions of the community are hindered by no durable obstacles from exercising a perpetual influence on society. In the United States the majority governs in the name of the people, as is the case in all the countries in which the people is supreme."

This quotation comprises a good introduction to some of the conclusions I have reached about American government in my own lifetime.

Power in the United States does rest with the people. Bureaucrats who think otherwise need to be told this repeatedly. Provisions of constitutions and laws guarantee the right of governmental control to the majority; but in the same documents may be found ample protections for minorities.

Regularly scheduled democratic elections make possible a new choice from time to time of representatives to govern in our republic. Persons we elect govern by and with the consent of those who vote and those who do not; of those who support, and those who oppose.

Our political party system, fluid and responsive over time to the changing needs of the people, serves us well. We are lucky not to have "class parties."

Government under law in America has been closer to the judicial ideal than the words of our radicals would have you believe. Our reformers have agitated for change; often, they have won their points. Administrators, meanwhile, who are often conservatives, have worked daily in our governments at every level and made our organized society one of the most envied in the world.

Citizens of other lands continue to be welcomed into the ranks of American citizenship. This means that as individuals—and as members of groups and of parties—they may participate in our system. They will find themselves included among majorities; they will often choose to stand with minorities.

Will they be like an Alexander Hamilton (first Secretary of the Treasury), born in the West Indies? Like Tom Paine (vital agitator for independence), born in England? Similar to Einstein the genius in physics, born in Germany? A labor leader like Matthew Woll, born in Poland? Or Wallace

Sterling, president of Stanford University [then], born in Canada? Who can say?

Those not born here, but naturalized (perhaps in ceremonies like this one) will be pleased if they at least become what we may call "the good citizen." The good citizen studies men and issues; he votes; he serves; he educates his children; he helps defend his new country in accordance with the Oath of Allegiance. You, as a new citizen, are more than welcome to join the rest of us as we try to build a social, political, and economic system appropriate to our high ideals and fervent hopes.

**** **** ****

AMERICA: YESTERDAY
AND TOMORROW

Delivered in the outdoor Lithia Park Bandshell, Ashland, Oregon, before an audience of about 1,500 on July 4, 1966, Independence Day). Printed in full on the entire editorial page of the Ashland Daily Tidings, July 8. The address was slightly edited when delivered on the classroom--later Semester at Sea-- ship Ryndam in April, 1969 to the student body of about 500 of the World Campus Afloat, an around the world university ship, when on the South Atlantic Ocean halfway from Capetown to Dakar.

America is a land that we know from personal experience and whose past we know vicariously. Residing as I do in the lovely old town of Ashland, Oregon, in a green valley surrounded by mountains, often snow covered, deep in the Northwestern United States, I feel a need to evoke a sense of our national history.

Speaking to that point, Woodrow Wilson once wrote, years before he became a national figure, "the past has made the present, and will make the future." Enlarging on this, he asked, "Shall we not constantly recall our reassuring past, reminding one another again and again, as our memories fail us, of the significant incidents of the long journey we have already come, in order that we may be cheered and guided upon the road we have yet to choose and follow?" If we will but study the past, said Wilson, study our history again and again, we may conquer the "rushing movement of affairs" and somehow form "an adequate image of our life as a nation?"

Is it not possible that from study of our national past will come understanding of our national character, and from assessment of that character today can grow a sense of wisdom about ourselves and some feeling for the probable future?

What *is* our Past? What has been the nature of our character as a nation? In a changing America in a changing world, will we live up to the best in our past? Man is denied the right to know what the future holds, but a great people, united into a great nation, ought to be agreed on what we want to take with us into the future.

It is a good time for assessment: our young men fight and die under the national emblem in a foreign land; our cities and our people are divided. Our universities have been in some instances akin to battlegrounds. Yet we walk briefly in space and circle the moon. *[1966]* We live with the computer; we dread thermonuclear disaster; we worry about overpopulation and underemployment. If ever we needed the perspective that can come from study of the past, we need it now.

The Child's Past. A portrait of our past is presented to us as school children. Here is the America of the Pilgrim Fathers, seeking freedom to worship in their chosen way;

of a William Penn honoring treaties with the Indians; of courageous Nathan Hale (and the weak Benedict Arnold). There is presented to view the towering figure of George Washington—an object lesson in self-effacement and integrity. Booker T. Washington, *W.* E. B. Du Bois, and Martin Luther King appear as pioneering leaders of the black people. Every school child absorbs the vision in the Louisiana Purchase, comprehends the patriotism of Patrick Henry and Daniel Webster, and is urged to emulate the lofty character of Lincoln--even Lee.

Yet all is not unity as we teach. In the South the children may learn of the events of 1861-65 as the War for Southern Independence (or the War Between the States), while in the North it was for many years the War of the Rebellion. In any case, most children accept the idea that it was "good" to save the Union, and it was "good" to free the slaves.

Other wars were to be fought and enter the books. In a few decades Americans proceeded to free Cuba. Filled with idealism, we helped to humble the Kaiser. Hitler, Mussolini, and Tojo were crushed by our armed might, but Stalin was strengthened. The first nation to join the United Nations, we defended the Free World in Korea under its flag. Mainland Asia after 1949 came to be colored red, as much of mainland Europe had been as the Iron Curtain descended. The integrity of Southeast Asia has come to be considered part of a related anti-Communist struggle.

Even youths know we are still challenged by the evil called Communism, whatever its form in various places. We all know there are awesome risks and possible penalties for courageously standing our ground on behalf of democracy.

Another Picture. Responsible members of the adult world accept much of the basic history of America, and we take pride in it. And why not? Our Declaration of Independence has been a beacon light to the world. The crucial words are familiar at home and abroad:

"We hold these truths to be self-evident—that all men are created equal; that they are endowed by their Creator with certain unalienable rights; that among these are life, liberty, and the pursuit of happiness; that to ensure these rights, governments are instituted among men, deriving their just powers from the consent of the governed."

These were revolutionary thoughts in 1776, although Thomas Jefferson thought them the common sense of the matter, and Thomas Paine used the word Commonsense to good advantage when converting those who hesitated. In many a country on this Earth in the 20th century the Document remains revolutionary. Much of American history in the years since that day has been concerned with achieving their deepest meaning.

The Constitution of the United States dates from 1787; as a political document it too has been influential overseas. Hand in hand with British Parliamentarianism it has been a guide for orderly self-government everywhere that leaders try to bring order out of chaos.

Our institutions—legislatures, executive branches, courts and laws, civil services—have defects, but they make daily self-government possible. It is the very absence of the civic machinery that we take for granted that makes life in much of Africa, Asia, and Latin America so trying an experience.

Americans need not apologize for basic aspects of an orderly society that grew out of their past. We mail a letter; normally it arrives (despite occasional delay). We dial across the continent and assume, almost always correctly, that our party is out if nobody answers. Who brags that he recently bribed a policeman or fixed a ticket in our society? We frown on such conduct. The level of honesty in local government seems to be rising, although there is certainly room for improvement.

The American record shows some greed and exploitation and even conquest of a kind that some historians insist on calling imperialism. Much of the land and many of its native creatures have been ravished; we are getting an environmental crisis. [I then taught a course on the matter.] The power-seeking and wealth-accumulation of yesterday's railroad barons we naturally prefer to describe as "the spanning of a continent." The enthusiasm for Manifest Destiny in the 1840s that led to the conquest of misgoverned Mexico and to the defeat of the primitive Indians we prefer to call a sense of Mission. The exploitation of the Negro's labor in slavery for more than three centuries was part of something that children a century and more ago called "a way of life." Yesterday's style in miseducation led many to believe the falsehood that the blacks among us were simply incapable of full participation as an American among Americans. The history of women was little noted until fairly recently.

Our true story, it turns out on close examination, is a real past of glorious moments and of some humiliations; yet overall it is a past to respect and, in thoughtful moments, to revere. We praise the achievements of Jefferson, of Emerson, and of Jane Addams. We ask youth to emulate such leaders. Yet we recall with a shudder the past of Andersonville prison, of more than 2,500 lynchings, tar and feathers, vagrancy laws, coolie labor, Pinkerton detectives and the rest. Haunted by all this, we hope to linger on quite different parts of our history.

The Old America. There was certainly an Old America. It was the America of our youth, of our parents, their parents, and theirs—on this continent and in the home countries. It was the America of the humanitarian Herbert Hoover, who worked his way through Stanford University, labored in a mine after graduation, earned a fortune as an engineer overseas, and ultimately devoted over half of his years to public service. It was the land of Thomas Alva Edison, the curious boy who overcame personal handicaps and invented the electric light and the phonograph.

That was the America of the defiantly independent Henry Thoreau, and of angry Eugene V. Debs, daring Brigham Young, inspired Mary Baker Eddy, and monopoly-detesting Robert M. LaFollette. These dissatisfied, critical, thoughtful, tough-minded, spirited, independent men and women were part of the Old America. There were puzzling figures then, like publisher William Randolph Hearst, who possessed strange combinations of competent professionalism and peculiar personal characteristics.

That America of yesterday was also the land—let us face it—of the poor house and the insane asylum; of patent medicines and child labor; of slums and ghettos and tenant farmers. The bleakness of migrant labor was visible, so too were malaria, pellagra, and hookworm. We did not then have the benefits of a nationwide vaccination program either. There was bigotry; there was violence. In the West there were land grabbers and claim jumpers, and in the South for a time carpetbaggers and hooded figures. In the colonial period there was indentured servitude as one path to freedom; there was *slavery.*

The facts of slavery have been retold repeatedly. Its legacy, and that of the war that both white and black men fought to eliminate governments that protected it and the new central government that was formed to preserve it, comprise a shadow with few highlights. The full history of the black man in America has been, nevertheless, one of accomplishment in spite of enormous psychological, economic, and political obstacles. We are only now [in the 1960s] beginning to sense the new black history in detail and comprehend its meaning. Much that can be said in all truth of the America of those centuries, especially on growth in democracy, hardly applies to those who picked the cotton, labored in the mines, and endured raw discrimination. These Americans gradually acquired skills, and many prepared to climb the heights as educated citizens and partners in nation-building.

Overall, we must say that there was in the Old America, compared with Europe and the rest of the planet, much *opportunity.* In comparison with others there was *freedom* (at least in the North and West). While the ideals of the Declaration were not realized, the direction of change can be seen.

There was the gradual forging of Democracy, and there was erected a great Republic and a pioneering Federal system. Free enterprise capitalism linked the continent by rail, telegraph, telephone, and then airplane. In time we built a structure of comprehensive government regulation and assistance, and created a vast welfare apparatus that began from churches and community financed groups and grew to include government at many levels. To be stressed is the fact that we built a pluralistic nation of voluntary agencies, service clubs, and religious bodies—truly noble organizations dedicated to service to their countrymen and to God.

There grew to be idealism, along with vigor, enthusiasm, and selflessness. Most of our leaders led with a sense of responsibility that is easy to recognize and should never be taken for granted.

We loved the land that we built. Walt Whitman understood that America and he wrote about it in words with muscle and compassion. Carl Sandberg sensed the spirit that was in the land. Our folk songs reveal plain folks who are, by turns, constructive builders or destructive critics.

The patriotic songs of the historic America are songs of glory, immense vision, and soaring spirit. They say that we are on our way; we have a vast and virgin land; we will be heard from. Our restless, opportunistic, ambitious, surging, and mobile people are to be a beacon light for the world. "Hail! "Hail Columbia, happy land!" "My country, 'tis of thee, Sweet land of liberty, Of thee I sing." "Columbia—the gem of the ocean, The home of the brave and the free." "Praise the Power that has made and preserved us a nation." And again, reference in time of war to the flag that still flies over "the land of the free and the home of the brave."

It was exciting to participate in the Old America. "From sea to shining sea" we were confident. We believed in Progress. In those years white male Americans, even recently naturalized immigrants, participated in self-government; others impatiently awaited their turn. Even so, a national character emerged.

The American Character. What will be our character as a people as we move onward toward the year 2000? What kind of people will the far more than 200 million human beings in the United States turn into with the passage of time? Each is, and will be, different from every other one—even in a mechanized, computerized, and organized age. Taken together, as a whole, we have had and may continue to have much in common.

We have been active—busy doing something. Work has long been central to our culture. We have admired the worker. Will we feel guilty with our long hours of forthcoming leisure? In the past, we have seen the world in moral terms. We have passed judgment on ourselves and others in terms of good and evil. Will our standards now sag to lower levels? Perhaps our new audio-visual aids can be used, if we wish, to give better and more enduring instruction in ethics and right conduct—of course without too much indoctrination or invasion of free will.

We are still a restless people, characterized by mobility. We move from place to place, state to state, North to South, East to West, and now overseas and back; yet we take pride in our roots and feel close to friends who share our place of birth. In the new urbanized and industrial age, will we stay put, or will movement become easier and routine?

The world has been learning, gradually (and somewhat reluctantly) that we are a humanitarian people. Often we profit from our generosity, no doubt, but sometimes we do not; and in either case the effort continues—after earthquakes, floods, and pestilence, and especially in war's terrible aftermath. We thought that whatever else was true about the appalling Vietnam situation, we would eventually rebuild the physical country better than it was before. The future on this is hard to predict. Will we continue in humanitarian pathways? Or will our growing experience of the world as it is sour us on the possibility of perfectability gained through sheer will?

Over the years we slowly conveyed full citizenship on women. While much of the world still has not done so, the struggle of women for still greater gains grows steadily.

Over the years we prided ourselves, prematurely and unrealistically, on our progress in the area of racial, economic, political, and social justice. We came to have riots, and division, and separation, and suspicion. Is this, then, to be our destiny? Is this all the great American experiment can produce?

As is true of other peoples, we have long loved our country, for the thing of beauty it has been, and for the symbol of freedom it remains. This love of country has been aggressive and unashamed. But some of our commentators and teachers carelessly slander the traditional patriotism while offering nothing to replace it. The badly divided United Nations has turned out to be, on the whole, unready for our love and esteem. [1966] Are we being set adrift?

We may not be able to preserve what is left of the Old America, for the forces of change are inexorable. We can try, and we should, to preserve what is best in the American character. Above all, we must control our destiny and not allow random inventions and unplanned innovations to destroy us.

The New America. Meanwhile, as we live through the 1960s, what of the New America? What of the life just ahead? Are we preserving, and passing on, the story of our heritage to our youth? Is this American history of ours to be a required subject in our colleges—or bypassed in a headlong rush to the sciences or to vocational subjects?

The life we once lived had opportunity, but not a guaranteed annual wage. It had expanding frontiers and job mobility—but not true job security, profit-sharing, and safety campaigns and devices. It had the thrill of success or the despair of failure, but not social security, manpower retraining, Medicare, or food stamps.

We Americans feel we have improved on the past. Perhaps we have; no doubt we had to. Certainly our life has been organized and regularized and sanitized. Our children and our aged appear to be more secure. These are not small accomplishments, yet there is a bill to be paid from taxes, and some freedoms have been lost.

As we look forward we hear new ideas, and we suspect some of them will modify our reality. What are some of possible changes ahead? [Beyond 1966]

1. Peak efficiency in business and government that will be achieved through systems analysis and with machines possessing fabulous qualities derived from transistors. Our previously untidy methods are supposed to be made perfect from dawn to dusk, apparently.

2. Use of income tax rebate machinery to guarantee every adult an income of maybe four thousand dollars or so as a matter of right.

3. Entitlement to a job, maybe to a contrived job like yesterday's WPA leaf-raking.

4. The right to free education through college, or loans to attend that get cancelled.

5. A right to "appropriate housing," and to a "proper" environment, and to live a life in unfettered "association" with one and all. What do such words mean?

6. For all humankind a right to peace. Also a right to survival to three score and ten. Nuclear weapons are to be developed that are "clean" and have no fallout, thus making feasible a new and vastly more destructive form of "limited" war. *[A vague reference to a new secret bomb the author learned about at RAND in 1961.]*

Is it unforgivable to suggest quietly that one cannot have some of these new rights without losing certain existing rights that were central to the Old America? Thus: will we be free in a possible age of total government—computerized and bureaucratized—newly expanded to bring the new changes? It ought to be something of a truism that the effort to bring new rights is likely to be destructive of existing rights. Even so, much is satisfying in these visions of change. But let us be cautious.

How high will be the price if we sacrifice values and habits that are basic to the life of free men? Our future lives will have a new pace and a new tempo. There will be ample time for reflection, of course, but will we be able to vote ourselves back to the *status quo ante* if we decide to change our minds?

The Opportunities Ahead. As we peer into the future, are we ready to say what it is that we want? What are our goals? What should we yearn to have come true? Surely we can be better than a ship of state without a compass. Here is a list:

Equality of opportunity; equal justice under law; full democratic participation; jobs for those willing to work; economic security for the individual; a bright light in the lamp of hope. These seem basic enough. The fact that they can be stated briefly does not lower them.

We want to keep, in addition, a right to privacy; a right to retain sizable amounts of our earnings from the tax collector; and the possibility of wholesome recreation in open spaces (even given our urbanization).

We seek to build a better American citizen: one more tolerant of differences in religion and race; more cultured in the humanities and the arts; higher in social understanding; more interested in carrying civic responsibilities.

In several areas of life we face immediate crisis, without much time to effect change. One is in race relations. Here, we want fair play, respect for those who are deserving of it, and compassionate attitudes toward those of whatever color who are overwhelmed by modern society. *[The following sentences were added for the 1969 shipboard version.]* Equal justice for women must be on our list of areas needing improvement. Until being a clerk ceases to be a lifetime plateau in employment we will need to put real effort into this.

Still another problem area is sexual license, in fact and in portrayal in words, pictures, and legal enactment. Here, the deterioration is massive already and deeply disturbing to all who hope for family stability and orderly development of the young. In addition, the threats to both health and normal conduct posed by misuse of drugs, widespread alcoholism, wholesale self-medication rooted in self-diagnosis, and pollution of the environment are all too obvious.

As we look at the planet, we understand a growing need for world law respected by all and for world organization in which all will participate in good faith. To the extent that laws and organizations in the world arena share the major values in which we believe, we will want to consider very seriously furthering such construction of international edifices and legal structures. We will always weigh the effects on our sovereignty and the power that might be gained by states that are less democratic and advanced than ourselves.

We have long said that we stand for peace among nations. It does need to be said that we have participated rather fully in many wars, some of them designed (we hoped) to end war or to guarantee future peace. Now the future has come to hold undreamed of weapons—an arsenal that is frightening and awesome. Perhaps modern technology will soon bring even limited wars to a screeching halt. (We thought at one time that the atomic weapon might do that!) In any event, we must work unceasingly for *peace* and try to find formulas that will satisfy honor and bring international justice—all without the clash of arms.

Freedom with Responsibility. We must ask whether patriotism is going to fade away gradually in our next America. Some of us have one foot solidly in the patriotic camp! An explanation will be helpful. In spite of all that has been written in condemnation of nationalism and patriotism—with supporting data only too true, it appears *[1969]*—I believe that there should still be room within each of tomorrow's Americans for *a decent love of country.* We should have respect for our heroes. We should take pride in our Nation's accomplishments—and why not? We should preserve the best of our traditions, continue to teach some filiopietistic history, and hold high our proclaimed ideals.

But, you may say, you seek world government now, and you prefer to turn away from our own patriotism and move toward that new frontier? There need be no fatal split here. We all know that world government lies far in the future (lacking upheaval from thermonuclear war). We also have a seriously divided world in which the United States often leads the forces dedicated to freedom for the individual.

Let us sum up. Out of a wilderness our pioneering countrymen of all races, creeds, colors, and national origins created a mighty nation of vitality, of strength, of fortitude, of excitement, and of spirit (especially of spirit). That spirit—of independence, of nationality, of solicitude, of generosity, of courage, of vitality—that spirit in some form still lives among us today. Our dream of freedom accompanied by security, brought about through personal responsibility in a democratic environment, ought to live on among us. Our viable nation must carry on at least until utopia raises its feeble head.

Once more, we think on the key words spoken here: *freedom, security, and responsible citizenship.* Such ideas are central to us. We do not and cannot look on them with complacency. It is proper to look back on the path we have taken (even with detours), assess what we have become, and emerge with self-satisfaction. It is permissible when doing so to make realistic comparisons with other peoples in other lands to retain perspective.

Ours is a nation which, more than most others (we often think), has combined freedom with responsibility. We have provided a vast measure of justice and opportunity. In the years to come [spoken in 1966 and 1969] we will want to continue to inspire our children to rally around the items of simple faith that are largely responsible for our best qualities. That faith is a monumental idea: It is that *man can be trusted with the government of himself,* and this alone is the path to happiness for us and for all of humankind.

**** **** ****

A HUMANE FOREIGN POLICY
IN A NATIONALISTIC WORLD

First delivered before a gathering of student members of our Rogue Valley's International Relations Clubs at Eagle Point High School, Oregon, in February, 1968. The text was somewhat revised in wording in the middle of the next decade (1976) for college classroom use. (Rereading this essay in a new century after so much has happened, and so much is happening, has been a fascinating experience for its author.)

Our world has long been organized into national states. The nation-state is now a fact of modern life. Human beings have chosen to band together in this way. In Switzerland, in Malaysia, in Malta, in France—wherever one looks—we see in action the results of this deep desire and real need of human beings. Something we call *nationalism* is manifested in state after state, although tribalism lives on. The world has long been like this.

Nationalism is a force in the world, for good and for evil. It might be said that people have needs—for food, for shelter, for safety, and for education. But do not forget that they also have the need to organize together in large units for common purposes. People feel very deeply on this subject. A state may tolerate its own illiteracy and poverty without dramatic counteraction, but it is unlikely to permit its flag to be spit upon, its borders to be invaded, or its ships to be seized on the high seas without response.

Foreign policy formulation must take other people's nationalism into account. We may feel that there is no sense in sacred cows roaming about in the midst of a starving people---as in India, and we certainly could have reservations about such a state spending to become a nuclear power. We may be certain that China's millions also have no need for vast nuclear capability and much need for tranquility and peaceful progress. We may deplore the tribal barbarities and fragmentation in Africa that is related to misery. We may wonder at the many months during which Egyptian soldiers, thousands of them, remained captive in Israeli hands, Pakistani soldiers are in Indian hands, and Israeli soldiers in Syrian hands. We may believe that only some form of birth limitation will save the planet's resources in the long run. We deplore the violence of Turkish, Greek, and Cypriot partisans in Cyprus. Why don't others see what *we* see and act as *we* would have them act, we ask? Why doesn't General Amin leave Tanzania alone? Why can't North and South Korea unite or live at peace?

Make no mistake. It is not usually logic, or analysis or rationality, or faith that rules men's higher affairs and governs their decisions in matters of such great moment. It is men's determination to exalt their own state—their "own kind"—and to reach self-fulfillment in this self-satisfying way.

In Vietnam, whatever else may have been true, the Vietnamese of North and South alike have been determined to carve out an *identity* for themselves. [1968] Doctrines of world unity must give way to this, it appears, and we need to take this into consideration.

Foreign policy formulation does indeed need to dwell on "human rights." Likewise human needs. And human desires. These are not at all the same. Dismiss from your minds, however, that we as Americans are free to do on the continents of the world those things which "experts" and "committees" and even professors and teachers come to agree would be good for human beings.

American foreign policy, in my view, has been among the world's most altruistically motivated. We deserve "A" for effort exerted. But the world does not award this grade. The world only understands a foreign policy based on national self-interest while expecting selflessness from the other guy! To others, our self-aggrandizing in Central America has been more comprehensible than our idealism in defending Korea or South Vietnam.

Do not drag the bottom of our historic policies for those instances of self-aggrandizement and aggression and mistaken purpose—and just stop there.

Look, rather, to those monumental actions of this great nation in foreign affairs. Look at, maybe read, Herbert Hoover's four volumes, *An American Epic* (1959-1964) in which he tells how we saved hundreds of millions of people from starvation (usually with Hoover's leadership) after two world wars. Read the record of the Marshall Plan, which saved Europe from chaos. Or consider our rehabilitation of Germany and Japan in material matters, and in spirit, at the close of bitter hostilities.

Ask (and be fair in answering) if our total policy since World War II has been aimed at the world's enslavement— or its liberation? Disregard for the moment insinuations about the CIA. Is it not correct that our policy is still that of President Wilson: the self-determination of peoples based on free, democratic elections? Note what Wilson said: "What we demand…is that the world be made fit and safe to live in; and particularly that it be made safe for every peace-loving nation which, like our own, wishes to live its own life, determine its own institutions, be assured of justice and fair dealing by the other peoples of the world as against force and selfish aggression." (January 8, 1918)

Do you wonder, now, that we produced the Truman Doctrine that saved Greece and Turkey; we negotiated the Soviets out of Austria; we stood fast in Berlin with the airlift; vastly helped to produce healthy new states in South Korea and Israel and Taiwan; and hoped to do so in Vietnam? It is not just our "anti-Communism" as the cynical world would have it. Nor is it Uncle Shylock conquering only to gain oil concessions. Rather, this nation, itself born free, seeks for others its own good fortune. It is because we ultimately responded to the slogan *Cuba Libre* that we feel so deeply the shame of deterioration into authoritarianism.

Speaking in Tacoma, Washington in 1919, Wilson gave postwar voice to that inner drive, that deep-felt need of the American born into a tradition of democratic republicanism. He said, "There is only one way to be an American, and that is to fulfill the pledges that we gave to the world at our birth, that we have given the world at every turn in our history, and that we have just now

sealed with the blood of some of our best young men."
(September 13, 1919)

Our foreign policies go beyond endorsement and furthering of self-determination, however. It was American vision that first dreamed of a League of Nations, and it was in San Francisco that the United Nations was born. In New York City it would have its being. Our money, far more in amount than that of any other nation [*But not per capita, etc.*], has financed major U. N. activities. It is not *our* indiscriminate veto alone that routinely cripples this hope of man for an end to aggression. [*US, USSR, and other states have used the veto. See Google's early entries for handy complete lists.*]

Unfortunately, the world has at large within it forces that do not share our hopes and dreams. These expansionist forces have been met and countered time and again. We now see that in expanding our military activities to prevent expansion by others it is *we* who lay ourselves open to the charge that we are imperialist.

We have indeed expanded over the years. In the 19th century we expanded across the Mississippi, and then to the Mexican border and to the Pacific shore. We went to Alaska, Hawaii, Puerto Rico, and for a time to the Philippines. We have occupied a power base in Okinawa and Sasebo. We have armed personnel in Northeast Asia (Korea) and Southeast Asia (Thailand). [1966] Our sixth fleet sails the Mediterranean and our uniforms may be seen in NATO countries. An American future in remote Diego Garcia, a mere dot in the Indian Ocean, is planned. [*This listing pertains to nearly four decades ago, of course.*]

Has the time come to pull back? Some think so. That action could open the way to the further penetration and expansion of Communist states. Then the frontiers of democratic self-determination and self-government would very likely shrink accordingly.

We see that our ambitious hopes for other peoples may have to give way before the redefined needs of our own society. Meaning no offense, it is apparent that the Swedes, the Japanese and the British, for example, quietly serve their own needs first and those of the world second. Any suggestion that we should do the same is met by outcries from many quarters that we would "betray our heritage," are "anti-Christian," or are "materialistic." It is so hard to admit that we may not be able to remake the world in what we believe to be our own image! Those who frame our foreign policies, however, have long recognized that elementary truth—whatever the public may naively believe.

Powerful we may be. Yet the world remains a huge place. It is a lot easier to fly over than to make over. Democracy may not prove the exportable commodity we think it to be.

Let us try to do our best. Let us base our policies on higher aspects of our heritage. Let us serve ourselves and those peoples that we can. Somehow, in so doing, we will have to avoid heartbreak at our inability to do everything rapidly. I would have us continue to try to do right; but this is as good a time as any to realize that evils have ancient roots and are widely distributed. There are powerful states that conspire to achieve their narrow goals—whatever the cost in human misery.

It will not be easy to sustain a humane foreign policy in a nationalistic world. Given our American heritage, however, I predict that we will continue to try. I know that our students, some of them leaders of the future, will make sure that to the extent of our resources and abilities we customarily will continue the long quest to achieve humane goals with our American foreign policy.

**** **** ****

AMERICA: THE LAND OF
THE DEDICATED

Delivered on Memorial Day, May 30, 1970, before Veterans organizations at downtown Hawthorne Park, Medford, Oregon. Martin Luther King and Robert Kennedy were killed a year earlier. I was speaking hard on the heels of the Cambodian incursion and the ensuing outcry on college campuses and demonstrations in Washington, D. C. and elsewhere. The text is the one delivered at the time, although several felicitous adjustments have accompanied the change from spoken to printed English. This speech dates from more than six and a half years after Tonkin Gulf and 16 months after LBJ left office.

These are spring days of great beauty. But they are also days of great concerns. We worry. We do not feel joy. The daily newspaper and the evening news on television bring crisis after crisis to our attention.

Perspective is hard to grasp, and imperfect as it is, it quickly slips away, leaving us bewildered.

Our worries compound and magnify. Strangely enough, we are not certain that we are worrying about *the right thing.*

I would speak for a time to this matter: What should we be concerned about? In these times of struggle and confusion, what needs our attention? As Americans, thinking about our "situation" on Memorial Day, 1970 we owe something special to those who have gone before—and particularly to those who have sacrificed themselves for our welfare.

What we owe is the duty to place our thoughts and our energies on what is important—to us now, and of significance to us and coming generations.

High on the list of meaningful concerns is mere survival. The human race has been threatened for a quarter century by the miracles of the Atomic Age: by weapons, possible fallout, and radiation. Even as we assemble here, weapons of awesome destruction are aimed at us. It is sobering to think about this. On the other hand, we recognize that those who govern us, and especially the President, can unleash vast destruction, even obliteration, on other peoples. We have known all that for a long time; we have become a bit numb; or maybe we forget; perhaps we just get diverted....

More recently, the threat to our planet, our home, our "environment" has brought special concern. The young people who must live out their lives in this threatening climate, and raise their own children in it, have this Earth as home. No other is available. Will it sustain life for their allotted 70 years or so? If the planet is to be grossly overpopulated, with resources depleting, will many perish altogether? Will living conditions for those who remain be so appalling that the survivors will envy the dead, as Herman Kahn put it? These are indeed gloomy thoughts.

On the one hand there could be thermonuclear oblivion; on the other, possibly, a pseudo-life on a tired and depleted land mass surrounded by lifeless oceans.

Small wonder that those who sense what could be are dedicating time, energy, and thought to preventing these awesome things from coming to pass. Surely, it ought to be said that some trends are being retarded and maybe reversed. Men of scientific competence, and leaders in public life who have great regard for young people, are making some impact on environmental problems. We do wish them well.

Perhaps it is not too late, after all! The SALT talks *[Strategic Arms Limitation Talks]* may turn out to be fruitful. For 25 years the Soviet Union and our nation have avoided Central War (the one what would dwarf all conflict previously experienced by mankind). The deterrence strategy has worked, so far, and we continue to rely on it. Yet we long for a day when the chemical warfare potential, and the atomic warfare potential, will join biological warfare weapons on the reject list.

Hopefully, this limitation of arms in future years will be by the Soviet Union and the Red Chinese as well as ourselves. Given their long professed attitudes toward us, we know—or certainly ought to know—that unilateral disarmament will never be a guarantee of our safety.

I spoke of other worries, of other concerns, ones that are subordinate to atomic-induced oblivion and environmental collapse. And it has been these other areas of concern that have so occupied our minds these past months: Vietnam withdrawal. The Cambodian campaign. Race conflict. Student activism. Constitutional crisis. We cannot fully address ourselves to all of these manifestations of the 1960s as we enter a new decade. Let us recall, instead, some of the basic motives that placed us in our present position, this spring of 1970.

It was on January 20, 1961 that youthful John F. Kennedy in his brief inaugural address (since proclaimed something of a classic) declared and promised on behalf of us all, "Let every nation know, whether it wishes us well or ill, that we shall pay any price, bear any burden, meet any hardship, support any friend, oppose any foe to assure the survival and the success of liberty."

President Kennedy pledged to old allies "the loyalty of faithful friends." We would help the people "in the huts and villages of half the globe…because it is right." Soon, on March 13, he would reaffirm in the Latin American nations "our pledge to come to the defense of any American nation whose independence is endangered." There ought to be, he declared, "confidence in the collective security system" of the Organization of American States.

Late that year (December 14, 1961), the President told Ngo Ding Diem in a letter that aggression in violation of the Geneva Accords would be viewed by the United States "with grave concern." We would "help the Republic of Vietnam to protect its people and to preserve its independence."

Two years later, in 1963, with reference primarily to the Soviet Union, President Kennedy said, "The United States, as the world knows, will never start a war. We do not want a war. We do not now expect a war. This generation of Americans has already had enough—more than enough—of war and hate and oppression." Our goal, he said, remained "a world of peace where the weak are safe and the strong are just."

In Southeast Asia, it developed, the goals of "peace" and of safety for the weak turned out to be incompatible. In a message to the Congress after Tonkin Gulf, President Johnson referred to an Eisenhower commitment back in 1954. That letter had offered our help in building "an independent Vietnam endowed with a strong government," one that could withstand aggression. Then there had been the SEATO treaty of 1955, which Mr. Johnson called a commitment and obligation. We keep our word, said Kennedy's successor.

The threat the American government saw was to many free nations in the region. Congress agreed on the threat, and we were on our way, ever more deeply. The Congress even proclaimed then, "The United States regards as vital to its national interest and to world peace the maintenance of international peace and security in Southeast Asia." All necessary steps, "including the use of armed force" would be devoted to assisting SEATO members and protocol states. The latter, it may be said, included Laos and Cambodia.

An event of that year on the home front had been the first Berkeley student revolt. And the 1960s were the scene of sharp and violent civil rights conflict. The hippies were born or rather created, and drugs made the scene. Meanwhile, we lived through Tonkin Gulf and bombed North Vietnam, the "Peace" button made its appearance on bumpers and lapels, and the television screen became a battleground.

At length we would stop the bombing; so-called peace negotiations opened in Paris; and the Nation was racked by political assassinations: "John, Martin, and Bobby" we said. The guitar and rock groups and the folk singers had their day. The generations in America were no longer on a first-

85

name basis, especially on campuses like, say, Columbia University.

Causes blended. There was "the war on poverty," and "freedom now," and "free speech," and "student rights." "End the draft!" "Rebuild the cities." "Stop inflation." "Relieve property taxes!" "Give the vote to 18 (or 19) year olds!" Hainsworth, Carswell. Fulbright. Agnew. "Stop pollution now."

Among all this there was a new President of all the people, Richard M. Nixon, who promised to "Vietnamize" the war and withdraw combat troops, and do these things in such a way that grave dangers to national integrity would be avoided.

In the spring of 1970, as all know, the President decided that our goals could not be reached unless Parrot's Beak and other "sanctuary" areas of Cambodia should be stripped of North Vietnamese war-waging material. Although Cambodia was the same protocol state for which we had long since expressed friendship, and one whose new government requested vast stores of arms, the critics of the war (and others) called this temporary campaign an *invasion* and set about the task of pillorying the President and a variety of other targets.

Universities erupted into violence. Distrust of the academic profession expanded in some quarters into hate. Demonstrations evolved by stages until at length Kent State and Jackson State became symbolic.

If the initial hope of Eisenhower and Kennedy had been to show that Communist aggression through guerrilla warfare and "invasion from the North" would not pay, by 1970 it was easy to say that they had not made their point.

But we *had sacrificed much*—perhaps far too much—for a small nation or two. Unlike Korea, there was no neat drawing of boundaries. Unlike Formosa, with its viable Republic of China, a similarly workable state might not emerge.

At home, it was "Hell no, I won't go." Faint indeed became the echo in memory of the Kennedy promise to "pay any price, bear any burden, and meet any hardship." The American people were tired: tired of the sacrifices, tired of the costs. Accustomed to fighting and winning, they were tired of limited war that was not limited enough and that did not promise victory.

Now [1970] we ponder all this. We remember the magnificent speech of General of the Army Douglas MacArthur (years earlier) with its refrain "duty, honor, Country." Thanks to television the war *for* the Vietnam peasants has come to look like war *against* native peoples. Abroad, we seek to negotiate with the Soviets and the Chinese; we try to settle the Arab-Israeli clashes; and we cooperate to keep NATO healthy. We have reached the Moon, and all humanity has thrilled at our technology and the display of heroism.

We pause: what in the world do all these events mean? Can we be both heroes and villains? Are we really waging *perpetual war for perpetual peace*? Have we devastated those we sought to help?

Moreover, in our own land has toleration of dissent led, perhaps temporarily, to toleration of open rebellion? Is this a real crisis we are in—a real revolution—or just another phase in the life of a free people living in a self-governing democratic republic? It had better be the latter! For we will not stand idly by while revolutionaries, white or black, young or old, well-meaning or not, bypass constitutional procedures. Revolutionary tactics will breed counter-revolutionary reprisal, perhaps partly accidental (as at Kent State), or virtual murder (as in Mississippi). *We must have no more of this.* Americans do not have the temperament for the politics of confrontation, especially where patriotism and order clash with idealism and impatience.

Now we renew the old struggle between President and Congress. The stakes may be high, but at least the game is played within the rules. This is what the veterans of our wars expect. They did not fight and get wounded and suffer (and see others suffer) so that their peaceful homeland would degenerate into a battleground.

Veterans are on both sides of the struggles inside America, wherever men of good will differ. But the veteran will not side with those who take the law into their own hands. The veteran accepts the lowering of the flag when it is a memorial to those who die: to the famous, to the heroes, and even to the very young who perish needlessly. The veteran does *not* accept the lowering of the flag as a symbol of real or imagined national misconduct. And he decidedly does not allow (if he can help it) the lowering of the flag as a concession to militants—whatever their proclaimed views.

Moreover, those of us who are proud to have served our Country, in uniform or out, continue to take pride in it. We regret that perfection escapes us. We rejoice that, on the whole, Americans "try harder" to befriend mankind than do some peoples. Ours is the spirit born of Washington and Jefferson and Lincoln and the Roosevelts, and especially that former Oregonian who saved over a hundred million people from starvation—the humanitarian Herbert Hoover. We must remember that great civilian on this Memorial Day, for he remains in the all time top five of the Americans most decorated, and Hoover is admired and remembered by the surviving peoples of greater Europe.

I have lost none of my pride in being an American. I deeply regret that not all of us see the issues in such a light; or that everyone can say the same. We seek, in Southeast Asia, to leave behind us at least four self-governing nations: South Vietnam, Laos, Cambodia, and Thailand. The goal may prove beyond us. But let the world bear witness that in the decade of the 1960s we tried!

Perhaps the effort will reassure those to whom we have extended promises of protection: the Koreans, Japanese, Free Chinese, NATO states, and the peoples of the OAS. We shield the Philippines. We now need to review those promises and gradually, through time, match our promises to our capabilities—and to our willpower. For we now know that some things cannot be achieved by a democratic state without descent into censorship, ruthlessness, and perhaps, the use of awful weapons---even atomic ones again…. Vietnam has been a hard lesson, and in some ways a valuable one.

The philosopher-statesman Woodrow Wilson in 1917 was correct, "the right is more precious than peace." Yet such a sweeping slogan now calls for sacrifice beyond the desires of far too many. Under the circumstances, we are just going to have to accept half a loaf (unless we are going to engage in constant armed struggle abroad—and, maybe, at home). This has been the message I offer you on Memorial Day,

1970. It adds up to these words: *understanding, patience, fortitude,* and continuing *commitment* to our friends abroad and our ideals at home. For this is America: still the home of the brave, and still, God willing, the land of the Dedicated.

**** **** ****

THE AMERICAN PUBLIC AND THE MAKING OF FOREIGN POLICY

A speech delivered in late 1970 when participating in a faculty panel at Southern Oregon College that focused on the above title. The event was part of the Fall Conference of Oregon Great Decisions (October 4, 1970). Edited somewhat in the next few years (I forget why) it is partially representative of the later 1970s.

Many in America at this time are convinced that because we went into Vietnam it is false to assert that "the public" has very much to do with the making of our foreign policy. The thrust of these words will be to the contrary. And I would like to attack a certain fuzzy mindedness that has surfaced regarding matters such as the nature of states, of power, and of presidential leadership.

States pursue power and enhance their self-interest. They are not charitable institutions. Can "the public" grasp this? What of those "leaders" who feel guilty when aiding the national interest and are afraid to use power?

The manner and extent to which the public is informed (or otherwise) is basic. Let me quote a paragraph from a distinguished and very widely read textbook, Thomas A. Bailey's *Diplomatic History of the American People* (1964 edition):

> "The American public is like a back-seat driver. It knows in general where it wants to go, but is not well enough informed to tell the driver—the Executive branch—precisely what roads or turns to take. These must be changed in Washington by implementing policies. And once the specific routes have been chosen, the public should be careful not to joggle the elbow of the driver by ignorant or misguided interference.
>
> "If the ordinary American wants to know who shapes fundamental foreign policy, all he has to do is look into a mirror. …The sovereign voter is ever at the elbows of the policy-makers in Washington."

While some want instant responsiveness from government, they are unlikely ever to get it. In my view they should not, for in some matters the experts do know better than the masses.

The time is now at hand, I think, for some of minority views (for example, those who favored "*Instant* withdrawal" from Vietnam regardless of consequences), to admit that they comprised a minority. "The political game" was not "stacked" against them. Present and future minorities should stop threatening and/or trying to intimidate the majority through words and deeds. The majority off-campus clearly favored *orderly* and *honorable* withdrawal from Vietnam, but this truth was nearly lost from view at the time.

Moreover, the ordinary citizen should admit that foreign policy formulation is not to be achieved in the bar or when bowling. Discussed, yes. Thomas Jefferson hoped the public could be educated to behave as responsible citizens. So far, so good. But the Jacksonian concept that anybody can fill any office and govern directly is hardly suitable to the 1970s.

We do need an *informed* public. We also need a far more modest, a humble, and a patient public.

I would like to pay my disrespects at this time to some normally silent intellectuals who in the 1960s abruptly or at least suddenly discovered the foreign policy area. Many of them obviously brought as their sole qualification in this exotic field a highly developed emotionalism and talent for raising their voices in righteous wrath. Some also express deep and abiding concern for every state and people— except our own. *[1970]* Still, it is from the American public that our statesmen and experts must come.

It is to that public that our leaders must appeal for support and understanding. Especially is this true when we pursue *long range* policies that appear down at the garage or barber shop to be "pretty darn stupid, if you ask me!" in the short run.

I worried most in recent years, perhaps, at the obvious unwillingness of some citizens to support their American Nation when it pursues policies with which they disagree. There is plenty of room for dissent, even when a policy has been agreed upon. However, dissent of such extreme (activist) intensity, or carried to such a degree that the state is weakened, can be a dangerous gamble.

Patriotism limped as a casualty out of the Vietnam Era. [Post 1975 opinion.]

Our foreign policy, whatever it may be, demands credibility from powerful states elsewhere. And credibility rests on a degree of unity achieved at home.

If I had been expressing myself at another time of great division, April, 1861, I should have said much the same thing. I would not then have let the "erring sisters" go in peace and thereby split the nation. And tiny terrorist minorities are not going to wreck the nation now. [ca. 1970]

Today's conflict within America is not sectional, and it is not entirely chronological (just one age group), and it is not necessarily a clash between "intellectuals" and those who punch a time clock or plant our crops. We do have a conflict, however, and it is far too heated and lacking in mutual understanding.

Those of us who try to teach others about American Foreign Policy perform an act of faith. We do not know whether our students will use their knowledge wisely, or one way or another. We must trust in their sense of equity, moral judgment, and regard for our body politic. We as teachers hope for the best, for it is all we can do. *We want to build an educated citizenry,* knowing that American Foreign Policy will be the ultimate beneficiary.

**** **** ****

IN MEMORIAM TO THE VIETNAM VETERAN

A Memorial Day address delivered at the American Legion Monument in the Mountain View Cemetery, Ashland, Oregon on May 31, 1971. Offered unchanged. (This entire book now seems to have this speech as its centerpiece.)

Near the top of our nearly mile high mountain pass, now filled with major highway Interstate 5 (a freeway that links Oregon and California) is a brass sign dedicating the four-lane freeway. All motorists who drive, hundreds of thousands of them, may read the words of memory placed there:

BLUE STAR MEMORIAL HIGHWAY
A TRIBUTE TO THE NATION'S ARMED FORCES
WHO
SERVED IN WORLD WAR II

OREGON STATE FEDERATION OF GARDEN CLUBS
OREGON STATE HIGHWAY COMMISSION

It is good for military men to be remembered in this way for service once rendered to one's country in a great war clearly fought for a great cause.

The reading of such sentiments reminds us of the habit of mankind to erect monuments to the heroic soldiers, sailors, and airmen of recent days who served in uniform and sometimes made the supreme sacrifice for their comrades, for loved ones at home, for Country, and (in a few clearly just wars) for men, women, and children everywhere, including those as yet unborn. Let us recall some of our past.

We remember those who fought and fell in the American Revolution in the successful effort to make a new and free nation that even in the age of kings would remain a democratic republic.

We remember also those who struggled in the War Between the States—the dead of both sides—who struggled for their homes or for the Union, in a war that finally freed the nation of the curse of slavery.

We remember those who perished in the cause of Cuban freedom as the 19th century drew to a close.

We remember those who went overseas in 1917 and 1918, never to return, filled with the hope that there could somehow be a war to end war, one that would make the whole world safe for Democracy.

We remember those who died in the Atlantic and the Pacific, in North Africa and Italy, on distant islands and the beaches of Normandy—all in the hope that tyranny once conquered would not rise again. We hoped then that Four Freedoms might bless all people in all lands and that the world would respect the new United Nations organization.

We remember those who did not survive in bitter cold Korea, fighting in the hope that the stubborn "police action" waged there would provide an object lesson and roadblock to expansionist Communism.

We properly remember all of our veterans on Memorial Day; we remember their Causes (for we teach about them in school); and we remember the heroism and the sacrifice and the glory of their eventual victories in battle. We remember their sense of honor.

We are aware, overall, that these men gave Americans a new nation conceived in liberty; and they stamped out slavery; and they brought independence to Cuba; and they twice crushed German militarism; and they set Japan on a peaceful democratic path; and they created a self-governing Korean state.

These are no small accomplishments for men (and women) in uniform to achieve in twenty decades.

In retrospect, we do deeply regret that those uniformed ones did not all return alive and well to their loved ones. Nevertheless, we are able to rejoice at their achievements. Always, we wish that mankind might somehow be able to gain great results without great sacrifices. This is not, however, the story of our national history.

So it is that at the top of the Siskiyou Mountains there is the plaque with a message of respect, esteem, and memory. Elsewhere—at Valley Forge and Gettysburg and national and state capitals are memorials.

Now we pause. For we gradually realize that among us are hundreds of thousands of new veterans of a continuing and controversial war, and that thousands who served will not return alive and healthy from that catastrophic war in Southeast Asia.

What memorial will we erect to the memory of these wounded and dead? What will we say in coming years about their Cause? Will we focus only on mistakes, misconduct, and misjudgment in our ranks and among leaders?

History tells us that there were many who bitterly opposed the Mexican war of 1845-46; but in the retrospect of years we teach that President James Polk and the soldiers of Scott and Taylor achieved their leaders' mission of extending the national borders from New England to San Diego.

Will we one day come to see clearly and to comprehend the dream of Presidents Kennedy and Johnson (yes, and President Nixon, to be fair) that oriental peoples are equally entitled to the inherent right of democratic self-determination and self-government? The temporary independence of Czechoslovakia once made us rejoice, and the creation of the Republic of Korea is now seen to be a worthy achievement. Will the preservation of a self-sustaining Republic of South Vietnam one day justify our high hopes? Meanwhile, the slow growth of self-government in an entire region populated by several hundred millions—from Indonesia to Burma—may turn out to have been the prize for which we fought a difficult and successful fight.

If all goes well (and it may), the Vietnam veteran will fare well in the history books, whatever the misgivings of this instant in the passage of time. In any case, those who fought against ruthless Communist forces in the 1960s were clearly on the right side in the long struggle for human liberty.

We should call on our leaders to begin planning now (it is by no means too soon) for suitable memorials to those who died in Vietnam. These memorials should be in Washington, in state capitols, and in our cities and towns. Is there shock or surprise at this call for an expression of national gratitude? [Kindly see the postscript to this 1971 speech.]

The war in Southeast Asia has not been a popular war! Still, the close observer would be overly partisan indeed if he did not recognize that our stubborn tenacity in this conflict has had meaningful results. There has been the preservation, so far, of anti-Communist governments in the theater of operations, and in Thailand and Indonesia as well. (Perhaps if these distant lands were European states we would better understand the full extent of this achievement.)

The manner of the fighting admittedly brought suffering to many thousands of innocent people. Some of our allies by no means exerted maximum effort. Side effects of the war have been debilitating here at home. The government of South Vietnam is not too far along the democratic path. But there has been overstatement in criticism.

If the Vietnam veteran is to be fully respected, and the Vietnam dead are to be rightfully honored, we must face squarely some myths and half-truths and distortions.

We have not, as national policy, taught our foot soldiers to kill helpless civilians—old men, women, and children. (Unfortunately, the instinctive killer in battle has long been part of the history of humankind. While we repudiate "savagery," we certainly differ over ethical questions in the waging of certain guerilla wars.)

Nor has our policy been genocide directed against the helpless. (Yet it is now evident that some methods of countering action in which we had confidence did not work out well in practice or always achieve their anticipated goals.)

It is not at all self-evident that it was contrary to international law for us to conduct military operations in Cambodia—which was then a state unable or unwilling to exclude the invading army of North Vietnam from maintaining effective and continuing belligerency deep within her territory.

In the Laotian civil war, the prolonged hostile occupation of portions of the country by North Vietnam was at length matched by temporary military action by partially American-assisted South Vietnamese forces. The outcry over these actions was emotional in the extreme and has been out of proportion. After all, North Vietnam has from the outset been the aggressor against three of its neighbor states (if we may here avoid debating the status in statehood of South Vietnam). This record cannot be changed. Already, the headlined events in Cambodia and Laos are being seen in some perspective, even by the most sensitive. As the smoke of battle gradually clears—especially as American combat forces continue to disengage—we approach the day for some assessment in retrospect.

Given some of the side effects of the Vietnam War— the upheaval at home, the openings given to Communist speakers and rioters in distant lands, the terror of new weapons and tactics, and the ghastly cost in men and money—there have been precious few among us to say it has all been "worthwhile." Quite the contrary. Even though there was justice in our original Cause, almost none will say at this time that things have worked out "about as well as might have been expected."

****

Postscript: It did not occur to the author until final editing of this book that my earnest public call in this 1971 speech for creating "suitable memorials to those who died in Vietnam" as "an expression of national gratitude" was a very early one. Not until 1979 was the Vietnam Veterans Memorial Fund, Inc. established. Jan C. Scruggs, Vietnam army veteran, determined instigator of the final memorial and hero of To Heal a Nation, was the initial donor and was squarely in the forefront of demands for a memorial in the late 1970s. Maya Yin Lin won the 1980 contest for a memorial design. John Wheeler, first chairman of the Fund, was in 1969 a captain in Vietnam; Robert Doubek, its project and executive director, was in 1969 an Air Force intelligence officer there; not until 1979 did Senator Charles Mathias, Jr. introduce legislation to authorize a site in Washington. President Jimmy Carter signed the bill on July 1, 1980.

Absolutely all I suggest from this recital is that my appeal from grassroots America was among initial calls for memorialization. Surely many sought, early on, appropriate public recognition of the service of Vietnam veterans. My call in 1971 was one of those issued (to a small audience) a decade and more before the actual legislation was signed.

**** **** ****

"WHEN OUR CAUSE IT IS JUST"

Delivered on Veterans Day before the large Medford Rotary Club at the Rogue Valley Country Club, November 13, 1973. The month was the tenth anniversary of John F. Kennedy's assassination. As the result of the Paris Peace Agreements, the last U.S. combat soldier is said to have left for home on March 29, 1973. The humiliating fall of Saigon lay two years ahead on April 30, 1975 when Soviet made tank 843 destroyed the gate of the Imperial Palace. The title of the speech is part of the famous fourth verse of the Star Spangled Banner: "Then conquer we must, when our cause it is just."

Before beginning my prepared talk, I must point out how contemporary is my subject. We have just witnessed the Congress taking momentous steps to curtail the power of the President to continue undeclared hostilities beyond a sixty day period. We have also seen our armed forces placed on limited alert in connection with Soviet efforts to protect the interests of her friends in the Middle East. We have read repeatedly of the massive buildup by North

Vietnam in the South, and of possible action to crush the Saigon regime.

The Cambodian conflict continues, and we wonder about its outcome. As the energy crisis deepens, there could even be voices raised in favor of adventurism directed at Arab states in the vicinity of the Indian Ocean. All in all, it is not purely theoretical to talk about possible future use of our armed forces in battles on behalf of what we believe to be *just causes*.

This year, 1973, marks ten years of my public speaking on patriotic holidays. The decade has been a trying one in which to talk about our national experience of war and peace. The Eisenhower years did not have prolonged episodes in our foreign relations that can be called "shattering." It was soon after his time when the Bay of Pigs fiasco and the Cuban Missile Crisis held center stage. Later came the Dominican Republic crisis and our apparent overreaction. Then arrived the era of prolonged war without victory in Vietnam.

At home, relations between blacks and whites deteriorated. We experienced appeals to seek out New Frontiers, a Great Society, and a New Federalism. As we flew apart over war in Vietnam, the President would seek in vain to "bring us together." New were calls for "the greening of America," and some even sought repudiation of the work ethic. Old moral standards were under frontal attack, for better or worse.

The decade brought assassination attempts, three of them all too successful. Now there would be disillusionment and other emotions. Civil disorder flared in Detroit and Watts, Kent State and Jackson State, and elsewhere. Later there was born something surprisingly controversial called "environmentalism." At length we entered an energy crisis. To cap it all, there emerged televised exposure of misconduct in the Oval Office, displayed in our living rooms virtually at entertainment levels. It was demoralizing. The chairman of the Senate Foreign Relations Committee would use the expression "arrogance of power." Still, foreign aid programs endured, though impaired.

Ultimately in world affairs we came to the point where we were headed out of Vietnam but not out of Asia. At the same time we became faced with a crisis of dangerous proportions in the Middle East. Keeping our policy of Containment [of Communism] we moved (to our surprise) toward Détente. Having confronted monolithic Communism for decades, we moved toward accommodation with Red China and peculiar new trade relations with both Mao and the Soviet Union.

We have very recently repeated, on a less dramatic scale, the "eyeball to eyeball" confrontation *technique* of the Cuban Missile Crisis. This time it was because of possible Soviet troop movements in the Middle East. We hoped we were not risking some kind of war, even of a "limited" type. *How far are we to go henceforth, we wonder, on behalf of allies and friends, agreements and understandings, treaties, and national honor?*

Overall, the American people are now declared by a Gallup Poll of this month to be lacking faith in their leaders, their institutions, and even themselves. Small wonder! It is in this most unpromising atmosphere that I have chosen Veterans Day as a good time to address you, a cross section of Southern Oregon leadership, on the enduring subject of war and peace.

*** *** ***

105

It is the language of the national anthem that provides my title: "when our cause it is just." My subject is the past and future choice between war and peace. Needless to say, so profound a subject as that choice expands the mind of man, for we must use imprecise words like honor, and duty, and right.

I shall be asking these questions: How old is the idea that we fight our wars for just causes? When war ends, should those who were its opponents join in honoring those who fought? There are still other questions. Have we praised too extravagantly the presidents who presumed that a good national goal fully justifies catastrophic war? Should we continue to withhold our praise from the presidents who decided that national honor can also lie in avoiding war?

Let's begin with the concept that military preparedness is an old idea. The case for keeping America strong was stated forthrightly by President George Washington in his Fifth Annual Address to the Congress on December 3, 1793:

> "I cannot recommend to your notice measures for the fulfillment of our duties to the rest of the world without again pressing upon you the necessity of placing ourselves in a condition of complete defense and of exacting from them the fulfillment of their duties toward us. The United States ought not to indulge a persuasion that, contrary to the order of human events, they will forever keep at a distance those painful appeals to arms with which the history of every other nation abounds. There is a rank due to the United States among nations which will be withheld, if not absolutely lost,

by the reputation of weakness. If we desire to avoid insult, we must be able to repel it; if we desire to secure peace (one of the most powerful instruments of our rising prosperity) it must be known that we are at all times ready for war." [Unless otherwise indicated, citations below are from various editions of Messages and Papers of the Presidents.]

Today, [late 1973] as we contemplate the awesomeness of modern weapons and reflect upon the apparent necessity of spending vast sums to keep the United States strong in the face of great power concentrated on the land mass of Asia, we might also do well to ponder the advice given by President John Adams. Faced in 1798 by an irresponsible France, he counseled the infant American nation not "to change or relax our measures of defense." Further, "...in demonstrating by our conduct that we do not fear war in the necessary protection of our rights and honor we shall give no room to infer that we abandon the desire of peace. An efficient preparation for war can alone insure peace," Adams told the Congress on December 8, 1798.

The goal of our second president was spelled out to be a harmony of measures which would "secure to our country that weight and respect to which it is so justly entitled." [Ibid., p. 265.] Moreover, "...nothing short of the power of repelling aggressions will secure to our country a rational prospect of escaping the calamities of war or national degradation." [Third Annual Address, Dec. 3, 1799.]

President Jefferson's two terms were years when there was dangerous conflict between Napoleon's French and the British. As he would soon be leaving office, Jefferson felt it necessary to give his countrymen some advice (November 8, 1808):

> "Considering the extraordinary character of the times in which we live, our attention should unremittingly be fixed on the safety of our country. For a people who are free, and who mean to remain so, a well organized and armed militia is their best security. It is therefore incumbent on us at every meeting to revise the condition of the militia, and to ask ourselves if it is prepared to repel a powerful enemy at every point of our territories exposed to invasion."

The idea of military preparedness we see in these words is as old as the nation itself.

President James Madison contemplated with dismay in 1812 the situation into which the country had passed with regard to Great Britain. In his Fourth Annual Message, November 4, 1812, he said the war [War of 1812] was being waged "not in violation of the rights of others, but in the maintenance of our own." Not to have met the challenge, Madison also warned,

> "would have struck us from the high rank where the virtuous struggles of our fathers had placed us, and have betrayed the magnificent legacy which we hold in trust for future generations. It would have acknowledged that on the element which forms three-fourths of the globe we inhabit, and where all independent nations have equal and common rights, the

American people were not an independent people but colonists and vassals. It was at this moment and with such an alternative, that war was chosen. The nation felt the necessity of it, and called for it."

Later, President Madison told the Congress the war was necessary "to assert the rights and independence of the nation." (Message of February 18, 1815.)

In the case of the Mexican War, it is worth noting that President Polk repeatedly said it was we who were *right*. There was a long record of "past wrongs" by Mexico. He quoted President Jackson as saying in 1837 that while such wanton outrages "would justify in the eyes of all nations immediate war," Jackson would recommend only reprisals for the time being. In any case, it was also honorable for nations to *avoid* war. By December 8, 1846, President Polk was ready to say, "The national honor and the preservation of the national character throughout the world, as well as our self-respect and the protection due to our own citizens, would have rendered such a resort indispensable." [Ibid., V, pp. 2324, 2326.] Polk soon noted that "every honorable effort" had been exerted to avoid war, but "the indignant spirit "of the United States had been aroused."

Lincoln was a critic of Polk's war. Yet at its close he found it possible to say of those who fell, "I think of all these brave men as Americans, in whose proud fame, as an American, I too have a share." [Quoted in Albert Beveridge, *Abraham Lincoln, I, p. 461.*] On this first Veterans Day after Vietnam [1973] we need to take this to heart.

Our Civil War was a terrible means to just ends, and our school books still openly admire the Lincoln who tried to replenish Fort Sumter at the risk of war. They view with contempt President Buchanan who absolutely would not do that. Buchanan said he saw his duty to be above all to preserve the peace: "this duty shall be performed!" *[Messages and Papers, VII, pp. 3189-90]*

For his part, Lincoln would risk war to preserve the Union and to execute the laws. "Doing this," he said in his first Inaugural Address, "I deem to be only a simple duty on my part, and I shall perform it so far as practicable unless my rightful masters, the American people, shall withhold the requisite means or in some authoritative manner direct the contrary." There would be no bloodshed or violence unless it should be "forced" upon the national authority. [Ibid., p. 3208.] What Lincoln really wanted, we ought to remember, was not war, and he did hesitate. "My countrymen, one and all," he said, "think calmly and well upon this whole subject. Nothing valuable can be lost by taking time."

That war was bloody. To Mrs. Bixby, mother of five sons who "died gloriously on the field of battle," Lincoln offered in 1865 "the thanks of the republic they died to save." (We still do this and must unite to do so.) Said Lincoln to the Congress July 4, 1861, the President cannot betray this trust, for there had been "no moral right to shrink, nor even to count the chances of his own life, in what might follow."

Contemplating late in the war the hundreds of thousands of casualties, the humanitarian President could even observe, "While it is melancholy to reflect that the war has filled so many graves and carried mourning to so many hearts, it is some relief to know that, compared with the surviving, the fallen have been so few." For the future, President Lincoln desired in his great Second Inaugural Address "a just and lasting peace among ourselves and with all nations." Here would be the fruit of war's sacrifice.

This extended view of Lincoln has particular value for our day, because it reveals clearly to our post-Vietnam generation the time a century earlier in which a terrible war was declared justifiable—a just war—despite its death and destruction. Such wars could be waged for both humanitarian and patriotic goals, with the ultimate objective, said Lincoln, "a just and lasting peace."

There is another point I wish to make, one indicated in the *Oregonian [October 18, 1973]*:

> "The Nobel Peace Prize has been awarded in the past to diplomats who have negotiated the end of wars. But the ideal would be reached if it were given for negotiations or other activities of statesmen which prevented the outbreak of hostilities. Unfortunately, such diplomatic tours de force often go without proper recognition."

Several examples come immediately to mind: John Adams shunning war with France, for example. Later, in 1896, as President Cleveland contemplated the insurrection by Cubans against the Spanish, he noted the "inevitable entanglements" of the U. S. with the rebellion. There was, he observed December 17, 1896, "a vehement demand in various quarters for some sort of positive intervention." Such a war, said its advocates, "could neither be large in its proportions nor doubtful in its issue." But, Cleveland said, our nation has "a character to maintain as a nation, which plainly dictates that right and not might should be the rule of its conduct." While peace is not a necessity to us, and we "wish to live in amity with all the world," war might someday be necessary. But first we should give "careful heed to every consideration involving our honor and interest" as well as the "international duty we owe to Spain." There would be no war.

*** *** ***

Another national leader who has not received credit for avoiding war—and for actively working against it—was President Herbert Hoover. When in September, 1931 the Japanese seized cities in Manchuria, Hoover called it "an act of rank aggression" in its direct, gross, cynical, and impudent violation of Japanese commitments. The "moral foundations of international life" must be upheld, he felt, so protests would be made and a "Non-Recognition Doctrine" on conquered territory was announced. He emphatically rejected enforcement of peace through the use of force or international boycotts.

Hoover (an old China hand) was then considered by his Secretary of State, Henry Stimson, to be "the best informed man in Washington on Oriental questions." He did his own thinking and he personally drafted all important public papers. A Hoover memorandum at the time said, "I felt that we must first make up our minds whether we were prepared to go to war" to support new international agreements aimed at Japan.

"If we were not we should take no steps that could possibly lead there. My own view was that war with Japan was unthinkable in our situation or for the stake we had in jeopardy. That after all China must defend herself; that if 300,000,000 people could not defend themselves from 36,000,000 it was hardly a moral obligation on our part to go to war in her defense."

In time, the Chinese would surely absorb or overwhelm the conqueror. "It might take fifty years, but for us to risk destroying our civilization, already in sufficient dangers, to speed this period up say seven years, was not particularly inviting." [Memorandum, undated, in Hoover to Stimson, June 3, 1936. Post-Pers. Indiv.-Stimson. Hoover Library.]

The Hoover Doctrine (sometimes called the Stimson Doctrine) did not restore Manchuria but it may have halted Japan's attack on Central China and induced their subsequent withdrawal. Some thought (and think) that the U. S. should have been more aggressive in 1931. Such persons would get their way in 1940-41 as embargos on scrap iron and oil shipments were a common excuse given for the Japanese attack of December 7, 1941.

Hoover would be a vigorous critic of President Roosevelt's handling of the prewar crisis, and in a press statement of December 8, 1941 the former president said, "I have opposed the foreign policies of our Government. I have believed alternative policies would have been better." [*Addresses Upon the American Road, 1941-1945,* p. 3.]

Much earlier, when President Hoover in mid-October, 1931 had been presented with the opportunity to utilize similarly provocative policies, he refused. He dictated a little remembered Memorandum on the subject of war, peace, and national morality. Said Hoover,

"The United States has never set out to preserve peace among other nations by force. … Our whole policy in connection with controversies is to exhaust the processes of peaceful negotiation. But in contemplating these we must make up our minds whether we consider war as the ultimate if these efforts fail. Neither our obligation to China, nor our own interest, nor our dignity requires us to go to war over these questions.

"These acts do not imperil the freedom of the American people, the economic or moral future of our people. I do not propose ever to sacrifice American life for anything short of this. If that were not enough reason, to go to war means a long struggle at a time when civilization is already weak enough." [Text in William Starr Myers, *The Foreign Policies of Herbert Hoover* (1950), pp. 156-60.]

This leader, Herbert Hoover, has been consigned to the peculiar oblivion reserved for America's peace-time presidents. "We will not go along on war on any of the sanctions either economic or military, for these are the roads to war," he said. Years later, he observed wryly that "he who brandishes a pistol must be prepared to shoot." Hoover said he would "fight for Continental United States as far as anybody but would not fight for Asia."

In summary, Presidents Adams, Jefferson, Cleveland, and Hoover were leaders who avoided the opportunity (in modern terms) to interpret "duty, honor, Country" in terms of belligerency. These peacetime presidents relied on "History" to justify them. "These are matters to be threshed out by History," said Hoover in 1941. School books have done little for any of them while glorifying wartime presidents like Wilson and Roosevelt who traded the title of peacetime President for that of Commander-in-Chief.

*** *** ***

What lessons can be drawn from this recital? As we emerge from the Decade of Vietnam, and gaze toward the Middle East [sic]; as we consider [spoken in 1973] our quarter of a century of freedom from major atomic and thermonuclear war; what attitude toward war and peace should we come to assume? How do we now behave as a moral state on the international scene?

First, we must maintain the reality of preparedness. Then, each Veterans Day we must continue to pay tribute to those who served and who suffered on behalf of the national honor. At the same time, we do need to pay our respects more fully, and considerably more often, I believe, to those Presidents who chose while in positions of leadership to walk the path of Peace and to carry the nation with them. And, we must be slow to go to war.

The expression "duty, honor, Country" does not inevitably demand or even imply resort to combat conditions or heroism in battle. National morality does not have to involve declarations of war or intervention in struggles half the planet distant.

What is it that we might wish for our people as we move ahead? Maybe, still, General MacArthur's words to those West Point undergraduates. That enraptured audience was a military one, and the advice was military. Today, the words need to be seized on as *peacetime counsel*. The path of duty, the upholding of honor, and the best interests of Country can lie in the direction of peace as well as war.

*** *** ***

I now return to the Wilsonian words "…more precious than peace…." Here is the eloquent context of those famous words:

> "But the right is more precious than peace, and we shall fight for the things which we have always carried nearest to our hearts—for

democracy, for the right of those who submit to authority to have a voice in their own governments, for the rights and liberties of small nations, for a universal domination of right by such a concert of free people as shall bring peace and safety to all nations and make the world itself at last free."

Also Wilsonian is the idea that we must fight for the right, a concept put into classic language by the man who led us into World War I, the man who said famously, "for the right is more precious than peace." (War Message, April 2, 1917.) Earlier when listing American rights, he concluded, "I cannot imagine any man with American principles at his heart hesitating to defend these things." (Address to Congress, February 3, 1917.) Such words had historic origins, as will be seen.

Somehow, in our Thermonuclear Age, and fresh in the memory of ten years of Vietnam, we need to find peaceful paths to reach such Wilsonian goals. We must reject the method of Wilson—and of wartime Presidents Madison, Polk, Lincoln, McKinley, Franklin Roosevelt, Truman, and the three presidents of the Vietnam Era—all associated with war. [*Written and spoken in 1973.*]

We may have to replace the outraged emotional short view for the thoughtful long view—essentially the method of Herbert Hoover. We must not pile evil upon evil while trying to stamp out evil. We must no longer, in the words of the caustic historian Harry Elmer Barnes, wage "perpetual war for perpetual peace."

American wars as instruments of national policy did in fact serve their assigned purposes. They brought Independence; preserved it; expanded the nation "from sea to shining sea;" and preserved the Union and freed the slave from bondage. Wars brought Cuba its freedom and crushed the Kaiser, Tojo, Mussolini, and Hitler; war contained Communism in Korea.

But the very logistics and weaponry of war are no longer as they were. (The Sherman of "War is hell" did not know the half of it!) Nor can the total consequences of modern wars be faced with the calm pride that, after all, *the right* has been served.

We need a new "War/Peace Ethic"—one which will be a blend of the war making and the peace-keeping activities of our national past; one which will leave room for praise of those who once fought for the right but are willing to fully recognize the legitimate honor in more peaceful paths of idealistic statecraft.

Ours is a nation rich in the memory of great leaders in both peace and war. We have yearned "to do the right thing." President Wilson could feel that America was "privileged to spend her blood and her might for the principles that gave her birth." Without totally rejecting that heritage, we must now stand also with Herbert Hoover on November 1, 1940 when as an ex-President he laid down some qualifications for another President during the grave days of 1940 [when Europe was at war]:

> "America needs a man who is truly devoted to the American Dream. That is a nation of free men—a nation of peace. It is the attitude of a President to the great principles of America that counts. If he truly believes in free men then a thousand of today's confusions find solution. If he truly believes in peace then peace will not be lost except by wanton attacks

upon us." [Salt Lake City speech, in *Addresses Upon the American Road, 1940-1941,* p. 255.]

While such an approach to world affairs may not place on heroic display an American leader lashing out against evil on all continents, or crusading with economic policies or armies in each matter under dispute, such an attitude may well serve as a corrective to the kind of global crusading that is now far beyond our means (and may be beyond our national will). The "just wars" of yesterday served their purposes. Let us admit it. But war can no longer be certain proof of national morality.

All in this audience believe in America. We believe that we must be strong and that we may have to use that strength, even now, on severely limited and infrequent occasions. But peace itself may now be the proper path to guaranteeing "the right." And we did learn in 1941 (or should have learned) that to take "all measures short of war" may well be just to guarantee an attack upon us. Faced with choices in foreign policy, we may never be able to be "neutral in thought and deed," for Wilson said presciently in 1915, "It is difficult for people to think logically when their sympathies are aroused."

Those who, like me, are still tempted to quote great Wilsonian phrases as guides for present action, might well bear in mind what that President remarked to his secretary shortly after the triumphant reception of his 1917 war peroration. He said, "My message today was a message of death for our young men. How strange it seems to applaud that."

*** *** ***

As the Korean War dragged on, President Truman's popularity dropped until only a fifth of our people thought he was doing a good job. Meanwhile, our memory of wartime President Johnson is still fresh. His crusade for freedom and democracy in Southeast Asia could not carry the support of all the public. Have we learned something from this traumatic experience?

Veterans Day, 1973 has been in my hands a time for taking stock of our posture toward war and peace and for remembering those who served in uniform in time of war. I have been at pains to recall the idealism of leaders who served the nation by keeping us out of war. How many are willing to join me in my major conclusion?

I urge the idea that we will best honor the veteran's memory if we are slow to act on the slogan of the National Anthem—words we sing often: "Then conquer we must, when our cause it is just." There is still merit in that. But we would be better advised to "Praise the Power that hath made and preserved us a nation." In the remainder of this century, I believe, we should be thoroughly prepared, but avoid war. We desperately need to rely on less militant—but still idealistic—means of upholding the national interest while upholding American morality.

While in past years the right was often thought to be more precious than peace—and that time may come again—the right may have been equally served when, with self-control and longer perspective, we sometimes kept the peace.

**** **** ****

IS THERE AN ETHICAL
ISSUE IN VIETNAM?

The initial version with this precise title was delivered as part of a panel on the Vietnam War sponsored by the Christian Ministry of Southern Oregon College on February 2, 1966. The present edited version was altered somewhat at war's end, so I am choosing to date it from 1974's editing, even though the changes were not major. "IS" supplanted "WAS" in the title, however.

Whenever some of Mankind assemble in an atmosphere of concern there can be an ethical issue. When people are surrounded with major issues of war and peace, kindness or brutality, love or hate, making of wounds or treating of wounds, educating in the truth or propagandizing falsehoods, thoughtful individuals will have to turn to their religion for ultimate guidance in ethical matters.

There is nothing new in this. War is not new. Brutality is ancient. Conquest and invasion began with man's ability to organize societies and build armies. Charity and philanthropy have ancient roots and have been practiced throughout human history. From Plato to Machiavelli, from Locke to Woodrow Wilson, mankind has reflected on the State, its sources, roles, and purposes.

Men have suffered from armies making war. But it was a time of upheaval, 1775-76, that gave rise to the lofty ethic of our Declaration of Independence. It was war that placed before our citizens selfless Washington, forgiving Lincoln, and (shall we say it?) the commanding Lee.

It is all very bewildering. We are aware of the 618,000 dead and wounded in our Civil War. We also know that it saved the Union to become the mighty nation that would lead the world in the 20th century and beyond. War facilitated the freeing from their masters of nearly four million slaves.

Napoleon made war; Napoleon was destroyed by war. The Kaiser invaded neutral Belgium and sank ships filled with civilians without warning, but war put an end to Prussianism. Yet war was definitely related to the ability of a Hitler to rise from obscurity; war demolished him and his creations. Out of war arose a Lenin and later a Stalin.

A League of Nations and a United Nations have grown directly from war. Few new nations have been born without violence in the vicinity. Few nations have survived very long—not Switzerland, not Sweden, not Finland—without arming men with weapons and teaching them to fight.

Born in the 19th Century, but gaining power in the 20th, a new evil, a coolly calculating anti-religious Communist ideology took upon itself the command of many states in the world, always fitting man to the Procrustean bed designed and refined by Marx, Lenin, Stalin, Mao, and the rest of a long list of ruthless ideologues.

When a Nazi Germany determined to conquer a continent and to try to erase a whole people, an aroused world suffered, bled, and died on behalf of ideology and nationalism while speaking vaguely of an international order to be led by them.

Dictators, men of evil, demagogues, and conquerors have amply demonstrated that they can mobilize humans on behalf of evil purposes. Faced by this, even the peace-loving Quakers have not been able to convince vast numbers of those with deep religious conviction that the proper response to evil is pacifism. World War II saw many members of the Society of Friends in some version of a military uniform, helping the war effort, unwilling to let evil triumph. They hoped that in time a peaceful world might evolve after defeat of totalitarianism, miseducation, and slavery.

We can now look back upon Vietnam, that tortured spot on the planet, [written early 1976] and we look hopefully for signs that Good and Evil were clearly defined and readily identifiable to those who undertook the long crusade by force of arms. We obviously hoped to conquer Evil—maybe with painless death, or with weapons that kill only the enemy, or with tactics and strategies that might miraculously give maximum results for minimum sacrifices.

We hoped that the ultimate outcome would be a viable Vietnamese state embarked toward democracy, prosperity, and happiness. We believed as we fought that in Asia, as elsewhere, the Communist ideology would prove unlikely to respect the individual as it rides what it has termed "the wave of the future." Surely it would lose.

We ponder in retrospect of only a year the use of violence by both sides. Jesus, we remember, drove the money changers from the temple using a whip. He stood squarely against evil in many forms. He was anything but quiescent about the world as it was. But violence was by no means basic to his nature.

I would not have anyone interpret what I have said here or elsewhere as praise of violence or war. What is portrayed is *human history,* in which war as a technique has played a large part—and not for goals that are always evil. We look at the big picture, thinking as Reinhold Niebuhr pointed out during World War II:

> "A catastrophic period of history may not create all the resources required for the solution of its problems; but it does finally destroy some false solutions and some of the inertial obstacles to advance." [*The Children of Light and the Children of Darkness (1944)*]

War, in short, because it involves terror and fear and bloodshed, is a form of evil. But war can give rise either to good *or* evil, or both. Much depends on which side prevails in the end. It is simply untrue that, as some say, "Nobody wins." Such a view is ahistoric in the extreme. Ask South Koreans if they wish that America had pulled out and let the Communists prevail!

Today there is little question that, in Niebuhr's own well chosen words during the war, the world is divided into "the Children of Light and the Children of Darkness." I am sorry to note that, somewhat as became the case with Hans Morgenthau, aged thinker Niebuhr hated, feared and comprehended Nazis then more than Communist expansion in Asia. He deplored extinction of the Jews, but he became resigned to the violent extinction of community leadership in the villages of Vietnam. I have concluded that he better understood the implications in the destruction of Western

SPEAKING UP FOR AMERICA

Civilization (1939-1945) than the disruptive effects of Communism on Asian culture and religion. I at least fear the doctrine born with Marx, expanded by Lenin, and exported by Stalin—and preached by Mao. It ranks with the evil fascist doctrines expounded by and placed into practice by Hitler and Mussolini.

There is condescension in Niebuhr's presumably off-hand description of Vietnam as a "small sliver of a nation with a peasant culture" which may be "incapable of either the democracy or integral nationhood which our dogmas attribute to it." South Vietnam, he said, may enjoy only "a primitive peasant culture." We do need to consider that. More important, when Christianity exalted the individual it is most unlikely that Asians got excluded from high hopes for the betterment of the individual. Was Jesus not virtually an Asian himself?

Niebuhr justified World War II in his book *Christianity and Power Politics* (1940). There he vigorously attacked pacifism and denied its validity in Christianity. Caustically, this great professor of theology at Union Theological Seminary concluded that those who would not support the battle against a Hitler-dominated Europe had eliminated all relative distinctions in history. He said they "praise the peace of tyranny as if it were nearer to the peace of the Kingdom of God than war." (p. 18)

Even the Quakers have presented a divided front on pacifism. There are indications that George Fox supported Cromwell's war against the Dutch. Although my own familiarity with the next point is enough evidence for me, it may not be enough for some readers. I quote from George Hedley, *The Christian Heritage in America* (1946), made up of lectures delivered at Mills College:

125

"In practice the Friends of today differ only relatively, on the war question, from other modern Protestant groups. Most of their young men have been willing, in the two German wars, to engage in noncombatant military duties: ambulance service and the like. Some have gone further, seeing these conflicts as of such compelling moral importance as to justify their full military participation. Others have maintained the old position in full strictness, refusing even noncombatant service. These last again are divided among themselves, between those who have registered for the draft and accepted assignment to the Civilian Public Service camps for conscientious objectors, and those who refuse even to register and therefore go willingly to prison."

There are those who view with ill-concealed contempt the confidence of some that a future of culture, decency, and even democracy could be postulated for the people of Vietnam. In addition, there were some in the 1960s whose confidence in America and her leaders was so low that they hated to think that our strength in the world might be increased if we prevailed in Southeast Asia!

To persons of either persuasion, I would only like to say, "Believe on the light, that ye may be children of the light." Was there an ethical issue in Vietnam? Apparently. But it was complex, and it will neither be resolved nor even clarified very much unless one has what may be called "a frame of moral reference." Is it too much to hope that men of good will can agree on such a matter?

Somehow, if history is any guide, we will continue to have Christian soldiers "marching as to war." At the same time we will have pacifists who say "thou shalt not kill" and who patiently wait for global evil to give way to ultimate good. We can expect these people to be laboring to ameliorate war's ravages.

My own views can best be summarized in the words of the Niebuhr of 1940:

> "If we are told that tyranny would destroy itself if only we would not challenge it, the obvious answer is that tyranny continues to grow if it is not resisted. If it is to be resisted, the risk of overt conflict must be taken."

And again, "Tyranny is not war. It is peace, but it is a peace which has nothing to do with the peace of the kingdom of God."

If the meaning of history is to some extent the story of the unfolding of human liberty—or if it ought to be—we must do what we can for the South Vietnams of the world. If we are to abstain or to fail, let it be because we *cannot;* not because we *will not.* In view of the ultimate Vietnam experience, however, where the hope to bring nationhood and democracy ran head on into the firm intention of the adversary to bring national unity and Communism, we will do well to avoid such military solutions henceforth. Although we could not (or at least did not) realize it in the mid-1960s, the final costs of modern war with bombs and defoliants and terrorist tactics—however unevenly distributed—are so extreme that the result can be unlikely to justify the means. The American Revolution did drag on for nearly a decade, and there was both disruption and pain. Comparison with post-war Vietnam suggests that our war for independence was vastly less costly than that in Southeast Asia—in casualties, destruction to property, and deterioration in the environment.

Finally, the question of good and evil, right and wrong, in connection with "just wars" now comes down to the matter of the extent of contemporary and future suffering necessary to bring ultimately beneficial results. Admittedly, this is no way to judge morality! In life, however, one must often weigh the costs against the consequences. In Vietnam it appeared that the consequences [that is, the rewards in self government] would vastly outweigh the costs. That turned out to be wrong (or it seems at this writing, [1966 and 1969] to be wrong. The time may well come [may one hope?] when more judicious attitudes will be directed toward all those who took strong positions on various sides of the intricate questions of supporting war, or resisting it, during the Age of Vietnam.

*** *** ***

AN ENDNOTE ON "THE JUST WAR." In my hardcover and paperback book The Presidency of Lyndon B. Johnson (Lawrence, Kansas: University Press of Kansas, 1983) there appears some 200 pages on the Vietnam War, including space (p. 282) on the matter of considering our effort in Vietnam "a just war." One source especially relied on in that place is an account by a professor of Christian Ethics that I considered particularly sound: Edward LeRoy Long, Jr., "What Makes a War Just?" Lecture at West Point. Christian Science Monitor, Feb. 10, 1981. Although I have gone back and reread my evaluation of President Johnson and the war that he and others waged in Southeast Asia, thinking to quote a number of pertinent paragraphs here, I have decided not to do so. The book has stayed in print about 27 years at this writing. It is readily available for purchase new or used or it may be consulted in a large number of libraries here and overseas. The literature that attempts to evaluate the Vietnam War is thoughtful and immense.

**** **** ****

REFLECTING ON PEACE AND WAR IN THE U.S. BICENTENNIAL, 1976

This essay was written in 1976 for the Bicentennial of the United States. The audience was students enrolled in a social science course, "The American System," and one other. While unchanged in content, this retrospective and analytical essay has been shortened slightly. Persons like me hoped all along that they were learning something out of the Vietnam experience. This speech opens with several paragraphs in which I try to explain to students at Southern Oregon College the rationale for my speaking out in public during the Vietnam Era.

The intellectual, psychological, and emotional climate in which my many speeches are being created is not easy to bring back to life. Some of us have a habit of trying to erase memories of unpleasant experiences. The worries, fears, apprehensions, and hopes of each year in the Vietnam Era should have been fully recorded in diaries at the time.

The expansion of United States troop presence in Southeast Asia in the early 1960s created apprehension among those familiar with warfare. The present writer was even more affected because he took so seriously the atomic threat to the U.S. That was because of my half year of editorial work on Herman Kahn's path making book *On Thermonuclear War* (1960). Central War (as opposed to Limited War) ought to be a topic for consideration at such times even if one would prefer not to be reminded of possibly catastrophic matters.

I considered it necessary in my patriotic speeches in the 1960s to remind representative elements among our then divided people that for years there had been underlying agreement on political and economic fundamentals. Even so, the developing phenomenon of quite open draft evasion (perhaps to Canada), and forgetfulness about our earlier aid to small states, offered themes to me. I gave an address to teachers on purposeful teaching of our American history. Our foreign policy was a frequent subject, since public disillusionment with it grew 1963 to 1975. I spoke to ethical questions involving the Vietnam effort, dwelling on the ethics of the effort more than the ethics of the methods being used.

Unremitting attacks on fundamentals on many campuses by the 1970s were influencing editorialists and greatly affecting this college professor. I spoke my mind!

Undeniably patriotic addresses such as these, revealing of self and offering answers to questions of judgment and appraisal, were anything but easy to prepare for public delivery in controversial times. I can recall, for example, some apprehension in May, 1971 that there might be a post-Cambodian invasion demonstration at my Memorial Day speech which, perhaps daringly, urged increased respect for returning veterans.

Notwithstanding, the ceremonies were always held as scheduled. As almost always, a tearful Gold Star mother or several could be counted on to leave early, maybe apologizing later. One long oration, part of a major July 4th commemoration, was printed in full by the local newspaper. One was delivered twice, the second time by request of a local radio station for its use. Press releases were seldom ignored; often enough they made page 1. There were no open attacks on content or aimed at the speaker—when in uniform or not.

Since it has become virtually impossible for a citizen in grassroots America to be noticed nationally, it is not a matter for surprise that there was no attention given to these efforts in distant Portland or San Francisco and not much thought given by me to the possibility. Gradually the high school bands stopped coming to those patriotic ceremonies. My wife, Beth Bornet, observed (maybe in 1970), "I feel as though we are watching the end of an era. Do you suppose there will be *any* observances of this kind in a few years?" We had to wonder. The audiences became chiefly the elderly from World Wars I and II. Korea and Vietnam were producing few audience members as yet.

It was then my judgment that in the 1970s there was little open appreciation of Vietnam sacrifices in the mass media. I nervously entitled my speech in 1971, "In Memoriam to the Vietnam Veteran" and spoke strongly and confidently to meet that need. (The day would gradually come when effort was made to recognize Vietnam services. Some organized effort would ultimately even be devoted by some to amnesty for those who had fled the draft!)

I do not doubt that most will find themselves reliving the turmoil of the Vietnam Era if they give these speeches a chance. That time was for some a period of drug addiction, rise in pornography, loud and abusive songs proclaiming new rights, domestic violence, artificial gaiety, political and constitutional strain nationally, and new concern of an environmental nature. Some leaders with a vivid memory of earlier wars that were brought to triumphant conclusions were in a sense cheerleaders for Cold War confrontation. Yet as we developed a mind frame akin to students of the decline and fall of Rome, we wondered how far along that road we had already come!

Like many, possibly, I am not entirely able to grasp or explain what happened to fundamentals that lodged in my thinking during those years when "America lost a war." The early 1960s may have marked the close of two centuries that might be called the "Age of Open Patriotism" in American history. We found ourselves by the 1970s in a "Post-Patriotic Age" of some kind. The Flag was still pledged routinely in schools, too routinely, and the hand was still over the heart at service clubs, but—to be flowery—the dynamism, the fervid spirit we once had, faded from the fervor of the past.

Some will approve of this development. If the United States should come to be attacked in war, however, our patriotic feelings may change abruptly. *[Written in 1976, oblivious, naturally, to the stirring events of 2001.]* It would take something of a miracle to bring back the emotional commitment felt by adults of 1918 or 1945. Possibly our patriotism henceforth will rest less on such matters as fervor, love, respect, habit, and memory. Replacing those things may come logic, enlightened self-interest, and scientific analysis of successes and needs in the international arena in times of stress. Helping others to avoid over-population and famine will require some self-sacrifice, and that in turn will require self-awareness, national self-effacement, and a somewhat different kind of patriotism.

**** ****

REFLECTING ON THE
MEANING OF JULY 4, 1776

A "Guest Column" published in the Ashland Daily Tidings for July 3, 1987 on page 4. The author had survived a devastating heart infarction in November, 1977 but still had managed to complete The Presidency of Lyndon B. Johnson in late 1983. The absence of Vietnam as an issue is to be noted. (Time had passed.) The text is as then published.

Once again we celebrate the Fourth of July. This time we are in a year in which our attention is centered on the 200th anniversary of the drafting of the Constitution of our country.

Summer, 1987, gives us the opportunity to think reflectively about the two greatest documents in our national history. It is the obvious truths that we most need to keep in mind.

The Declaration of Independence is chiefly to be remembered for its proclamation, in 1776, of certain truths then called "self evident," and its sturdy announcement that some of the British colonies had clearly given birth to a new nation.

The Constitution was designed in 1787 to create, in the name of The People, a new form of representative government that would guarantee political and economic stability without threatening individual or group freedoms.

Great names come to mind as we reflect on these towering documents. We associate the Declaration primarily with the figure of Thomas Jefferson, for he was the prime mover of the three committee members authorized to draft it. The Constitution, on the other hand, became the work of a variety of individuals assembled from 12 of the 13 "original" colonies. As we single out some from among the 55 who attended—the figure of James Madison always comes first to mind—we do some injustice to other thoughtful individuals.

Properly to be identified with both documents, of course, are the towering figures of George Washington and Benjamin Franklin.

The date July 4, 1776 is, perhaps more than any other, symbolic of rebellion against arbitrary, unconstitutional authority. This is true, no matter how much any who value order in society over other characteristics may try to minimize the revolutionary nature of our beginnings.

The Declaration itself is a study in contrasts. The chasm between complaints over "taxation without representation," and endorsement of such ideal conditions as being "created equal," possessed of "inalienable rights," and entitled to "life, liberty, and pursuit of happiness" well illustrates both the immediate concerns and the ultimate hopes of the drafters and signers.

On this date we may recall, at least when in school, other specific complaints of the colonists that led them to violent revolt. Some of the abuses then enumerated were overstated—a common enough practice among those with deeply felt grievances. Today, our time is better spent in contemplation of the idealistic hopes and dreams spelled out in hot and humid Philadelphia for the benefit of a then quite inattentive "candid world."

Those who signed the Declaration were fond of peace, beyond doubt. Still, it was absolutely their intention to engage in an all out fight against "tyranny"—even to the extent of waging war with ill-equipped armies during appalling weather conditions. They were determined at all costs to achieve the final result they sought: national independence.

At the time, there would be many solid citizens who were decidedly unwilling to break with the "mother country." The allegiance of those Loyalists was primarily to the British Crown; they would cling to current stability; and they would disregard charges that King George III was engaged in usurpations.

A small minority then (as today) certainly favored peace at any price. Suppose they had prevailed?

In any case, the revolutionary era in America was to be characterized by a divided citizenry. Although emotional spokesmen like Sam Adams, Patrick Henry, and Tom Paine reached out, touched, and convinced a great many, others remained unpersuaded to the very end. Today, we normally focus only on those who did prevail.

Our celebration on this date needs to be historically based, should it not? July Fourth may not be the most appropriate time to introduce a multitude of today's political, international, and emotional concerns, trying to influence one's fellows. Such efforts may readily backfire, when resented.

All who keep fresh in their minds the story of the birth of our Nation, who are aware of the risks once taken and the noble sentiments then expressed, will not hesitate to display "old fashioned patriotism," however briefly, on this day.

Here is a national event on which we can honor the members of the Continental Army who once fought (for gloomy years, as it turned out) to win the independence that had been so majestically—and optimistically—proclaimed in the Declaration.

Only in 1783 was the war to be formally concluded. The new state, after a shaky beginning, would be enduringly constitutionalized with the drafting of an improved written framework for future government in 1787; the beginning of self-government in 1789; and final approval of the Bill of Rights in 1791.

We will be thinking, as summer unfolds, of the whole sequence of events that transpired from 1783 to 1791.

If we are happy on this occasion, with parades and holiday spirit, it is not simply in anticipation of parties, pleasure in mingling with relatives and friends, or enjoyment of fireworks. We certainly can take great satisfaction at living through another beautiful day whatever the perennial threats to our environment and to our very survival.

When we fly our flags, we can remember that a train of historical events began in the 1770s. Among these were the beginning of American national independence; expansion of freedom for many (but not all) under the new government; and the development of an orderly society in which to work and live.

As we consider in our homes and our schools what to tell the members of a new generation of Americans about this patriotic holiday, we may want to use the past to mold conduct in the present.

From the American Revolution can be learned the great consequences that can flow from courageous sacrifice of self, comprehensive educational preparation of leaders, and the importance of seizing the moment.

That was a time, 1775 to 1789, when the ideas and actions of comparatively few citizens made all the difference to their fellows. The long arm of that generation of uncommon men would have an incalculable influence on all humankind in the two centuries that followed.

**** **** ****

HAVE FAITH IN AMERICA

Written in 2008 to be an entry in a Military Officers of America (MOAA) national essay contest for members. Not the winner, it was revised to this form in 2009. Much was on the writer's mind: the outcome in Vietnam;, the apparent close of the Cold War; the nature of the first Gulf War including Saddam's retention of power; the attack on the United States on September 11, 2001; the Second War against Iraq; the on-going effort to achieve goals in Afghanistan; the War-like activity against Terror, the unrest in our Hemisphere; China's growing strength; and the prospects for nuclear proliferation from North Korea and Iran. The perceived need—and my call--is for a mindset that includes patriotism.

I am proud to be an American citizen. There is no country I admire more than this one. Our military record shows that our country fights for good over evil. In World War I, for example, we tried to make the world Safe for Democracy; we supported national self-determination in Europe; when the war was over we fed millions of starving people thousands of miles from our shores.

In World War II the United States fought against tyranny and racial barbarism in Germany, Japan, and Italy. Infamous dictators were crushed; a holocaust was bought to an end. Our use of atomic weapons to win a final victory over Japan and save the lives of fighting men is controversial, but our motive—to prevent unbearable additional wartime sacrifices from our young men—should be understandable. That intercontinental war, rooted in a surprise attack on us, brought devastating casualties among Americans, and it took productive years from the lives of some who are still among us. When the struggle was finally over our long effort to contain Communist expansion in a Cold War began in earnest.

A democratic and free South Korea exists today because Koreans and Americans sacrificed in war together. An American president, Ronald Reagan, once ventured to call our long Vietnam War struggle "a noble effort," but it evokes mixed memories. Our purpose in the Vietnam Decade was to bring democracy to Southeast Asia, to protect free and independent states, and to prevent Communism's evils from spreading to South Asia and worldwide. There is a record of some success, but there were failures too.

The American military has been used to counter disasters and for good causes. It saved the Union in the devastating warfare of 1861 to 1865 as the North prevailed. World War I proved a catastrophe for winners and losers alike. Dictators were eliminated in World War II; then both Germany and Japan became democratic during and following our military occupation. Half a century of Cold War worked out better than many expected at the time. Korea became a free and independent state, but similar effort a decade later failed to establish freedom and democracy in South Vietnam. Panama and Grenada are better governed because we intervened. We prevailed in Kuwait and temporarily subdued Iraq; then we took on Iraq again from different causes and helped build a new state, but the end is unclear. We have helped establish a safer society in some of Afghanistan, but much remains to be done. One special goal we have had overseas--equity for women--has been hard to see through to enduring success, and the effort to induce worldwide good health has been uphill. We continue to negotiate to minimize the planet wide threat of nuclear weapons.

This nation volunteered foreign aid of various kinds for many generations and it still does, relying on both our government and private bodies. On balance, our voluntary organizations and the American government have made a huge difference with the non-military aid they have rendered in many forms after wars, in peacetime, and when catastrophes strike. The value of our aid in armaments is difficult to quantify, however, and it clearly needs rethinking. While perfection in our overseas activities escapes us, we continue our efforts to do the right thing. It is not surprising that we sometimes fail, sometimes in the harsh light of world attention. In the public and private sectors alike, we stay the course and often try to react in a timely way to criticism.

It is easy to demonstrate that our national homeland has a multitude of problems, many but not all of them economic. Sometimes we do not face them squarely, and there are inequities in the burden felt by different generations. Admittedly, at home and abroad our leadership and offering of resources to others has sometimes fallen short, so goals do not get realized. Nevertheless, the fair-minded among critics ought to be able to agree that our classrooms and leaders can give this venerable Nation a ringing verdict. Without hesitation I willingly assert: *We have long been, and we remain overall, a good and a great Nation.*

At home and abroad we have long expressed lofty goals. As we work (sometimes in vain) to fulfill them, we have every right to refer to our United States of America with pride. I am doing so now as I dare to stress the positive and place the negative in a subordinate position. What America has achieved for the good in several centuries of its existence is truly monumental. Casual words of praise do not begin to cover the need to appreciate what the United States--far away in the Western Hemisphere--did with enormous sacrifice for Europe and Asia during and after global wars.

We should look upon the symbols of our national sovereignty with affection. Our flag, our anthem, and our Great Seal stir our emotions, and indeed they should. I am confident that vast numbers of Americans, native born and newcomers alike, fully agree that we are entitled to display routinely a patriotic emotion similar to that shown at the very beginning of our national history by our Founding Fathers.

*** *** ***

A REFLECTIVE AFTERWORD

I no longer remember all of those who invited me to deliver these patriotic speeches. They included leaders of the American Legion, the Veterans of Foreign Wars, chairpersons of committees appointed to commemorate patriotic holidays, a representative of a federal court, and academic figures—all from Jackson County, Oregon. Those who invited me expected that I would speak for those once in the American military who were no longer among the living. Even though only a Reservist in those early Vietnam years, I still felt a veteran's empathy for the dead who were once in uniform.

I resolved very early not to turn my speeches into an argument over the growing conflict in Southeast Asia. To pass judgment on leaders is inevitable and customary, but as it happened I didn't need a speech venue to do that. A decade later I delivered my conclusions on the war leadership of President Lyndon B. Johnson, at least, in a large book that evaluated his time in office, *The Presidency of Lyndon B. Johnson* (1983). There I was free to pass judgment unreservedly, for the editors of the American Presidency Series of the University Press of Kansas mandated that from the authors it chose to put under contract.

147

I wished also to bypass debating the decision of our post-WWII presidents and Congresses to contain the spread of Communism—although I fully supported it. Today, the central aspect of the Cold War itself has not vanished, for a vast array of thermonuclear weapons are still programmed in our direction by Russia. We modernize our defenses, even as we negotiate arms control. Nuclear proliferation is an issue for Americans, and several new nuclear powers give concern, while those seeking future power are threats on a shrinking planet. *The world is the way it is. The alert will shudder and adjust.*

I am glad I made the effort in those dark days to speak formally to the general public about patriotism and the rationale for sending our military personnel far away and into danger, despair, and (many now say openly) to military defeat. That can be debated from various aspects. Those who then and earlier wore the uniform of the nation in combat deserved, I felt, tributes well beyond what I was able to offer. Nevertheless, I prepared well and did my best on these patriotic holidays.

A historian's word about performances such as mine is warranted. Patriotic speeches delivered to live audiences are seldom published. They tend to be overlooked by historians. There have been a few compilations by speakers in America and England. Over half a century ago a Wisconsin intellectual historian and friend, Merle Curti, wrote in his solid book *The Roots of American Loyalty* (1946) that our Fourth of July orations have been little utilized by those who study our past. "An intelligent and understanding patriotism," he suggested, will help a democratic state to survive. The United States had become "a hope for those in

all lands who longed for freedom and a democratic world."
(pp. 256, vii)

What I said about America seemed well received—whatever the turmoil of the times. Though the name *Bornet* was routinely listed in the phone book, I got no hate calls or mail. This is not surprising, for I was not speaking as a political partisan but as a patriot…. *These are not campaign speeches,* and the events were not rallies. Sometimes I used language calculated to arouse emotions--but never hatred; there is no call here for overt *action.*

There is need for sophisticated handling of the sometimes snide remarks made today about the crusade to establish a democratic Vietnam. Yesterday's verbal battle lives on! I should like to repeat what I said in closing my remarks at a Christian Ministry symposium (early 1966): "Surely the time has come…for more judicious attitudes toward those who took conflicting positions on these intricate matters in the Age of Vietnam." We do need a certain quietude in this new century when passing judgment on that generation, on its hopeful yet hard-pressed leaders, and on its tragic war. Indeed, the anti-war ardor of yesterday's war protestors needs to be placed in full context to be understood fully in our own day.

The anti-patriotic among us sometimes descend to portraying the United States in the role of an "empire" engaged routinely in "imperialist" invasions and dedicated to "conquest" for only "economic gain." Some proclaim that we should cut back on patriotism, especially in the schools, claiming to see "powerful reasons for that." *[Richard W. Miller, political philosophy professor at Cornell University, in "Unlearning American Patriotism," in Theory and Research in Education, 5 (2007), pp. 7-21]* Even so, they urge caution when combating patriotism, for one's anti-patriotic effort may turn out to be not worth stirring up a backlash in communities. Clearly, detractors have found patriotism a long lived, sturdy opponent.

A profound truth can be pondered and brought into in the open about our soldiers, sailors, airmen and others: Never far from their minds when overseas has been the happiness of their fellow citizens back home. Even as I write, another large contingent of the Oregon National Guard departs, with local publicity, for dangerous duty overseas. They will soon live with the hazards involved when, as citizen soldiers, they wage war. Some will die in a place hard to find on a map. Meanwhile, we are threatened in various ways by terrorists!

A final word as we close: Those who defend us, military regulars, reserves, and national guard alike, absolutely deserve the words of thanks we offer on national holidays. As contingents of brave personnel assemble at an armory and march away--soon to take risks for us--concerned citizens may murmur as always, "God be with them."

I say we should be proud to exclaim at the same time (patriotically, as did so many of our ancestors from the very birth of the United States of America):

"Hats off, the flag is passing by!"

**** **** ****

SOME OTHER WORKS BY THE AUTHOR

California Social Welfare (N. Y., Prentice Hall, 1956)

Welfare in America (Norman, Ok., University of Oklahoma Press, 1960)

Editor and author, The Heart Future (American Heart Association, 1961)

Labor Politics in a Democratic Republic (Washington, D.C., Spartan Press, 1964)

Edgar E. Robinson and Vaughn Davis Bornet, Herbert Hoover: President of the United States (Palo Alto, Ca., Hoover Institution Press, 1976)

The Presidency of Lyndon B. Johnson (Lawrence, Ks., University Press of Kansas, 1983)

An Independent Scholar in Twentieth Century America (Talent, Or., Bornet Books, 1995)

Leaders and Issues at Southern Oregon College, 1963 to 1980. 21,000 words, SOU Website. (Google this title.)

SPEAKING UP FOR AMERICA (Bloomington, IN., iUniverse, 2011).

Articles in such journals as: The American Archivist, Bulletin of the American Association of University Professors, The Historian, Iowa History, Encyclopedia of the American Presidency, Encyclopaedia Britannica Yearbooks, Presidential Studies Quarterly, Inter-collegiate Review, Pacific Historian, College and University, Journal of Negro History, Florida Historical Quarterly, Western Political Quarterly, Annals of the American Academy of Political and Social Science, The Freeman, and others. In the 21st Century there have been various articles on the Internet's History News Network.

THE AUTHOR'S LIFE

An Oregonian since 1963, the author grew up in Bala Cynwyd, Pa. but graduated in 1935 in Miami Beach, Fla. He earned the B.A. (With Honors) from Emory University in 1939, the M.A. in 1940, and spent a graduate year at the University of Georgia. He began Navy service as Yeoman First Class in World War II, was commissioned, completed NTS(I), Quonset Pt., and served three years as Barracks Officer, NAS Alameda. He retired as Commander, USNR. After faculty membership at Mercer University and University of Miami he got the Ph.D. (History) from Stanford University in 1951. The next decade he researched on grants and with nonprofits (Institute of American History (Stanford); Commonwealth Club of California, Encyclopaedia Britannica, Ford and Volker Foundations, American Medical Association, The RAND Corporation). Back in academic life, he was Chairman, Social Sciences Division and Professor of History and Social Science, at what is Southern Oregon University. He has been awarded three civilian medallions for "distinguished service." Dr. Bornet served 20 years on the Oregon Committee of the U.S. Civil Right Comission. The author's career is sketched in Who's Who in America since 1957 and Who's Who in the World since 2006. He and his wife Beth W. Bornet, long a recognized volunteer, made their home on a forested hill in Ashland, Oregon. Their daughter Barbara Bornet Stumph lives in Walnut Creek, CA, and their son Stephen Folwell Bornet resides in Stamford, CT.

*** *** *** ***

LOVERS IN WARTIME, 1944 to 1945
(San Ramon, CA 94583, dvs Publishing, 2016)

HAPPY TRAVEL DIARIES, 1925 to 1933
(San Ramon, CA 94583, dvs Publishing, 2017)

A RESEARCH HISTORIAN'S CONSTRUCTIVE
LIFETIME (San Ramon, CA 94583, dvs Publishing, 2017)

Printed in the United States
By Bookmasters